Jessie Willcox Smith

Jessie Willcox Smith

S. Michael Schnessel

Thomas Y. Crowell
Established 1834
New York

Library of Congress Cataloging in Publication Data
Schnessel, S. Michael.
    Jessie Willcox Smith.
    Includes bibliographical references and index.
    1. Smith, Jessie Willcox, 1863-1935.
NC975.5.S64S36   741.9'73 (B)   77-3530
ISBN 0-690-01493-7
Printed in Great Britain

Acknowledgements

Building a book is like building a house. You can't do it alone. I wish, therefore, to thank the following persons who gave of their time and effort to help in the completion of this volume, either by providing personal information about Jessie Willcox Smith, by offering material for photography, or by giving me access to files and papers in their possession.

Dr. Francis Adler; C. Douglass Buck, Jr; Mr. and Mrs. W. Keen Butcher; Mr. and Mrs. John E. Cline; Mrs. William S. Crowder; Mr. Richard P. DeVictor Mr. and Mrs. S. Hallock DuPont Jr; Mr. and Mrs. Benjamin and Jane Eisenstadt; Miss Edith Emerson; Mr. and Mrs. Morris S. Emory; Mr. E. Thomas Flood; Mrs. Ruth Garfinkel; Mr. and Mrs. Thomas S. Gay, Jr.; Mr. and Mrs. Herbert J. Goldbloom; Miss Carolyn Haywood; Mr. and Mrs. Julian Lapides; Mr. E. B. Leisenring, Jr; Mr. Horatio G. Lloyd Jr; Mr. Ken Mazik; Mr. James Kirk Merrick; Mrs. James S. Merritt Jr; Mary Griffin and Barbara Wilson of Paper Moon; Mrs. Samuel H. Paul; Mr. and Mrs. Corning Pearson; Mr. Pierre M. Purves; Mr. Marc Schoettle; Mr. John Schoonover; Mr. and Mrs. Edwin S. Sheffield; Mr. and Mrs. Winston C. Sheppard; Mr. and Mrs. James H. Stevenson III; Mr. John H. Thompson Jr; Mr. George F. Tyler; Mr. and Mrs. Harry F. West; Mrs. Arthur L. Wheeler; Ms. Ellen Winans; Miss Jessie M. Wissler; Mr. Art Wood.

I also wish to thank the following institutions and companies and their staffs for their assistance. The Delaware Art Museum, Rowland Elza, Phyllis Nixon, and Catherine Stryker; The Brandywine River Museum; The Pennsylvania Academy of the Fine Arts, Elizabeth Bailey; The Library of Congress, Stepanie Munsing, Jerry Kearns; The Free Library of Philadelphia, Robert F. Looney, Diane Kazlauskas, Louise Floyd; Newman Galleries, John Liddel; the New York Public Library, Princeton University Library; Little, Brown & Company; Good Housekeeping; The Ladies' Home Journal; Dodd, Mead & Company; Procter and Gamble; American Standard, Inc; the American Red Cross; Houghton Mifflin Company; David McKay Company; Archives of American Art.

Special personal thanks to Catherine Connell Stryker for her helpful catalog, "The Studios at Cogslea," [Delaware Art Museum, 1976) whose Appendix materials were an important aid to this volume; Christine Huber, whose catalog for the Pennsylvania Academy [The Pennsylvania Academy and Its Women,

1973) provided important background for this work; Dominick N. Procaccino of The Exhumation for help with research and important encouragement; James J. Kery for his guidance and patience; Kathryn LeVan for her help as deadlines approached, and to any others who helped and whom I have shamefully forgotten to include in this listing.

Picture Credits

5, 6, 7, 8, 9, 10, 73, 74, 78, 79, 80, 81, 82, 83, 94, 95, 96, 97, 98, 99, 100, 101, 132, 133, 134, Good Housekeeping; 4, 73, back cover, Benjamin and Jane Eisenstadt; 11, 12, 19, 20, 23, 162, 163, Mrs. William S. Crowder; 15, Ellen Winans; 16, 22, 92, Edith Emerson; 17, 18, 21, Rare Book Department, Free Library of Philadelphia; 45, 46, 47, 48, 49, 50, 56, 59, 60, 61, 68, 69, 70, Dodd, Mead, & Company; 48, 49, 50, 59, 60, 61, collection of The Library of Congress; 51, 52, 58, Little, Brown & Company; 62, 63, 64, 66, 72, 76, 77, David McKay Company; 72, Mr. and Mrs. Edwin S. Sheffield; 105, 128, 129, 130, 131, The Ladies' Home Journal; 109, John R. Schoonover; 114, The Brandywine River Museum; 131, The Pennsylvania Academy of the Fine Arts; 136, Campbell Prints Inc.; 138, The American Radiator Company, Inc.; 139, American Standard, Inc.; 140, The Cream of Wheat Company, Inc; 142, The American Red Cross; 144, The American Library Association; 145, Corning J. Pearson; 146, Mrs. Winston C. Sheppard; 148, Dr. Eleanor Scott; 149, Mr. and Mrs. James H. Stevenson III; 150, Mr. and Mrs. Morris S. Emory; 152, 153, 154, 155, 156, 157, Procter & Gamble, Inc; 158, American Radiator Company; 159, The Philadelphia Welfare Federation; 161, Mr. and Mrs. Harry F. West; 5, © The Hearst Corporation, 1921; renewed, 1949; 9, © The Hearst Corporation, 1921; renewed, 1949; 10, © The Hearst Corporation, 1930; renewed, 1958; 24, © Bobbs-Merrill Co., 1907; renewed, Edmund H. Eitel, 1934; 28, © Harper Brothers, Inc, 1909; renewed, 1937; 65, © Duffield & Co., 1923; renewed, Ada M. Skinner, 1950; 67, © Duffield & Co, 1925; renewed, Ada M. Skinner, 1952; 78, © The Hearst Corporation, 1926; renewed, 1954; 79, © The Hearst Corporation, 1929; renewed, 1957; 80, © The Hearst Corporation, 1929; renewed, 1957; 81, © The Hearst Corporation, 1931; renewed, 1959; 82, © The Hearst Corporation, 1929; renewed, 1955; 94, © The Hearst Corporation, 1918; renewed, 1946; 97, © The Hearst Corporation, 1930; renewed, 1958; 99, © The Hearst Corporation, 1932; renewed, 1960; 101, © The Hearst Corporation, 1930; renewed, 1958; 105, © The Curtis Publishing Co., 1912; renewed, 1940; 128, © 1908 The Curtis Publishing Company. Reprinted with permission of Ladies' Home Journal; 129, © 1908 The Curtis Publishing Company. Reprinted with permission of Ladies' Home Journal; 130, © 1908 The Curtis Publishing Company. Reprinted with permission of Ladies' Home Journal; 131, © 1908 The Curtis Publishing Company. Reprinted with permission of Ladies' Home Journal; 160, Mrs. L. M. C. Smith.

Contents

Introduction
For the Love of a Child

URING her prime years as an illustrator for magazines and children's books, Jessie Willcox Smith achieved a popular and financial success which far outweighed that of any female predecessor or contemporary. Yet Smith had been raised in a rigid Victorian society where women's roles were clearly defined, a society where a single woman was lucky to earn her own living, much less make thousands of dollars each year.

Had the Pennsylvania Academy of the Fine Arts in Philadelphia, founded in 1805, been any less advanced, and had Smith not had the later advantage of studies with the forward thinking Howard Pyle, it is quite conceivable that Jessie Willcox Smith would be a name unknown to American illustration.

This remarkable artist began her career at a time when many significant advances had been made in the teaching and general acceptance of female artists. Her native city of Philadelphia, despite its rigid social climate which was so overly concerned with protocol and class standing, was among the most advanced cities in the world with regard to artistic opportunities for women.

In Philadelphia during the early 1800s, numerous "drawing academies" had flourished; primarily due to an influx of British artists who had come to the United States after the American Revolution to seek a viable means of income. The emphasis at these academies was primarily on amateur accomplishment and not on professional training. Young ladies who attended these classes were generally from the wealthier levels of Philadelphia society, and their artistic efforts were viewed as merely another stage in the development of a well-rounded debutante. If they accomplished nothing else these early drawing academies-cum-finishing schools at least cleared the way for other art schools with more serious intentions and programs for women.

The few women who had achieved some fame as artists in the early 1800s did so mainly with help from male family members who were already established artists themselves. Jane Stuart, the portraitist, had the wisdom and experience of her father, Gilbert, to guide her. Jane Cooper Sully Darby, also a portraitist, was the daughter of Thomas Sully. Similarly, Anna Claypoole Peale, miniaturist and still-life painter, came from a family of artists, including her father James Peale and her grandfather, James Claypoole. All these women had the benefit of professional training in the home and personalized criticism for their artist

Five · little · maidens · all · in · a · row
And · each · is · trying · her · best · to · show
How · big · she · is · from · top · to · toe ·

1. "Five Little Maidens All in a Row," *St. Nicholas,* May, 1888. Jessie Willcox Smith's first published illustration

relatives, not to mention access to their supplies, libraries, and art collections. But few women had such advantages. Even the prestigious Pennsylvania Academy, though it permitted women to exhibit in its annuals, did not accept female students until 1844.

However, the 1800s were alive with changes and many advances after 1840 promoted women's entry into various endeavours previously closed to them. Scientific inventions like the industrial sewing machine played an important liberating role. Many women who formerly made their own and their families' clothing were now freed from that task thanks to the availability of store-bought clothes. As various industries expanded a demand for the skills and labor of female workers and artisans began. This demand for artisans and designers prompted Sarah Peters to create the School of Design for Women in Philadelphia in 1844, the institution where Smith would begin her art studies. Similarly in New York City, the Cooper Union-Free Art School for Women was founded in 1859. It was also during the late 1840s that the first women's rights convention was held at Seneca Falls, New York. The age of Women's Liberation had begun.

"What a country is mine for women," wrote Harriet Hosmer, the most successful female sculptor of the mid-nineteenth century. "Here every woman has a chance, if she is bold enough to avail herself of it, and I am proud of every woman who is bold enough. I honor every woman who has strength enough to stand up and be laughed at if necessary. That is the bitter pill we must all swallow in the beginning; but I regard these pills as tonics quite essential to one's mental salvation."[1]

Hosmer understood well the problems facing career women in that era. Despite the opportunities that lay before them, success in any profession demanded a dedication and determination beyond the powers of most women.

2. "Little Puritans," *St. Nicholas,* December, 1901, a later illustration which shows the influence of Howard Pyle

REPINE - NOT

JESSIE
WILCOX
SMITH

4. "Mother and Child" from *Dream Blocks*, 1908, oil and pastel

Even at the Academy women artists who wanted to expand their artistic awareness had to fight for the right to do so. Women had not been given the opportunity to draw from live models at the Academy prior to this time. While male students were permitted to draw the nude male and female figure, women were at best allowed to copy plaster casts of Greek and Roman statues in the Academy's statue gallery. Even then, men were not permitted to be present at the same time and fig leaves had been tastefully attached to all the male statues to prevent the lady artists from being exposed to indelicacies.

So in 1860, three years before the birth of Smith, a dissident group of female students at the Academy formed a life class independent of the school's faculty and administration. The students took turns posing for each other and, even though they modeled clothed or partially clothed, this bold defiance of Academy policy caused a considerable stir in the prestigious art school. But these ambitious young artists would not relent. They demanded and eventually received the same rights and privileges as their artist brothers. While this tale of rebellion and victory may seem tame by today's standards, where almost unimaginable deeds have been done in the name of art, this organized protest helped to open the doors for major developments which enhanced the role of women in American art.

Cecilia Beaux, the noted Philadelphia portrait artist and the first woman to receive the Academy's prestigious Gold Medal, understood the ways in which society restricted women artists during the mid-1800s. At the turn of the century,

5. Cover illustration for *Good Housekeeping,* November, 1921

6. Cover illustration for
Good Housekeeping,
June, 1925

she looked back at the previous decades and wrote, "Women in the past have lived an intensely subjective life. Everything that life held for them depended so entirely upon their qualities as women that it could not be otherwise. They have not had the power of expressing themselves objectively like men. But that may not hold true in the future. With the multiplication of opportunity women are getting a training that they never had before . . . Out of this mass of material a great artist may be produced."[2]

In all fairness to Philadelphia though, one must admit that the women's art life there was more advanced in the mid-1800s than it was in many cities, including Paris. "You can't poke fun at Philadelphia to an American artist nowadays," said Cecilia Beaux. "The Quaker town holds too honorable a place in the brush world."[3]

Yet despite its several opportunities for art education, Philadelphia still had to defer to the magnetic draw of Paris which was irresistible to young artists of the day. Mary Cassatt and Thomas Eakins, among the Academy's more famous graduates, both left Philadelphia in the mid-1860s for continued study in France. Eakins was immediately taken under the wing of the Ecole des Beaux-Arts, but Cassatt had to be content with copying paintings in the Louvre and paying for private lessons. Women were simply denied entry to the best Paris art schools of the time. Even the prestigious Academie Julian did not open its doors to women until 1880, more than three decades after the Pennsylvania Academy had made the same liberal move.

Such restrictions did little to help the female artist's view of herself. Foremost among her problems were feelings of self-doubt. Even Mary Cassatt felt strong pressures from her family, and when she exhibited her work it was as Mary Stevenson for fear of embarrassing her family should she use the Cassatt name. Almost all women artists were convinced that only certain subjects were appropriate for them to paint – still lifes, landscapes, children, and maternal scenes. Historical, allegorical, and mythological scenes were thought too challenging for their limited experience. Regina Armstrong, a critic and writer, once wrote of woman's role in the nineteenth century, "She has been regarded somewhat as the disease of civilization, much in the same manner that the pearl is said to be the disease of the oyster, – and held as a precious bauble of inutility."[4]

Yet even with the social pressures working against them, science was working for the female artists and for artists in general. The invention of the collapsible tube, for example, revolutionized the use of oil paints. Painting on location became easier and faster, and artists were no longer burdened by having to carry bottles of solvents and other chemicals for on-site painting.

Even more important was the development of photography, and its eventual use as illustration in the late 1880s. Photographs were quickly replacing the tediously prepared and expensive wood engravings that had been until this time the most economical, realistic image possible in the periodicals of the day. Artists and engravers no longer had to copy life with precision. Photographs were doing it for them, and illustrators and artists could now apply themselves to the artistic and subjective aspects of their work, to seeing what the camera could not see. After the novelty of the photograph passed, interest in the work of individual illustrators increased once again. The personality of the artist and his or her interpretation of a work became as important to the publications of the day as the stories they printed.

Periodicals of the late 1800s had already opened their doors to female illustrators and many eventually established strong reputations and followings. Mary Hallock Foote was appreciated for her scenes of the American West; Georgina A. Davis, a staff artist for *Frank Leslie's Illustrated Newspapers,* was an early chronicler of domestic scenes. Maud Stumm was best known for her illustrations for the classic Greek and Latin poets; while Maud Humphrey built her strong reputation on her illustrations for children's books. There were many others – Rosina Emmett Sherwood, Marie Guise Newcomb, Matilda Brown, Alice Barber Stephens, and Florence K. Upton, to name a few – and they were only a handful of the dozens of women artists who established sound careers as illustrators in the 1870s and 80s.

It was in the light of these developments that Smith began her career as a young art student. This tall, shapely, good-humoured young woman was in many ways a product of Philadelphia society and its models. The perfect society woman was expected to be refined, well read, soft spoken, and graceful. Before her eventual marriage to an appropriate suitor of good family and considerable means, she could assume a profession considered suitable for a young lady. Perhaps she would teach grade school before entering college. Smith certainly fulfilled many of these social expectations, although she never married. Her parents were not "Main Line" Philadelphia, the epicenter of the local high society. They had instead migrated to that city from New York. Yet even though their names were not listed in the Philadelphia Social Register, the pressures for Smith to conduct herself in a model way were as strong as if she had been born into the Philadelphia elite.

In keeping with her family's expectations Smith, always a lover of small children, prepared herself for a career as a kindergarten teacher, a profession considered quite suitable for a young single woman in 1883. But Smith, soon after becoming a teacher, learned that reality sometimes falls short of the ideal. While giving her a regal appearance, her tall figure was also a disadvantage when it came to dealing with youngsters. She was continually bending down to serve her young charges, a situation that left her with a tired and aching back at the end of each athletic classroom day. She often remarked that the physical

7. Cover illustration for *Good Housekeeping,* January, 1928

JANUARY 1928

25 CENTS

8. Cover illustration for
Good Housekeeping,
April, 1928

discomfort she suffered in her chosen career quickly led her to a side door which opened to her career in art.

Smith had shown no inclination to art as a child or as a student. She did, however, have a female cousin who was an amateur artist of some ability. A young professor had asked Smith's cousin to help him with his drawing lessons, and Smith joined them during the first lessons. It was not long before it became obvious which of the three had the greatest artistic talent. Smith's modest sketches were received with such enthusiasm that the lessons became a regular affair. The young man retired from this pleasant avocation at an early stage, but Smith received immediate support from her friends and her family after her sketches were revealed to them. She was permitted to leave her teaching post and in 1885 she entered the School of Design for Women in Philadelphia.

Aware of the many women of the period who earned their livings from the pages of the popular periodicals, Smith focused her studies toward a career as an illustrator. At the time, of course, she hardly realized that she would find such an important place in the annals of American illustration. Directing her sights toward such a career was a courageous move. In her own family and among her friends at the time there were no models for her to follow.

Smith was obviously determined and not easily discouraged. She quickly realized that the School of Design for Women was laboring under a long-established history as a crafts and finishing school for ladies. Embroidery, textile weaving, and lace making may have been practical subjects of study for women who would do no more than decorate their husbands' homes, but they were not suited to a woman with greater career hopes. Within a year, Smith transferred to the Academy where she studied with Thomas Anschutz and the volatile Thomas Eakins, her first major artistic influences.

But Smith was destined to have an even more important mentor. After two years at the Academy, she attended the first class in illustration at the Drexel Institute of Arts and Sciences, also in Philadelphia, under the direction of the well-known author/illustrator, Howard Pyle (1853-1911). His influence changed her art and her life forever.

An illustrator and teacher, Pyle was founder of the Brandywine school of American illustration, and his teachings lay the foundation for such greats as N. C. Wyeth, Frank Schoonover, and Maxfield Parrish. Smith often praised her instruction at the Academy, but she freely admitted that at Drexel it was Howard Pyle who "simply blew away all that depressed atmosphere and made of art an entirely different thing."[5]

Pyle was no ordinary teacher. If he had faith in a student's ability, he would obtain commissions for that student from publishers in New York, Philadelphia, or Boston, the American publishing centers of the time. He was immediately taken with the talents of Smith and her friends and fellow students, Violet Oakley and Elizabeth Shippen Green, all who developed impressive artistic careers. Smith and Oakley owed their first major commission to Pyle who recruited their dual talents to illustrate an 1897 edition of Longfellow's *Evangeline* for the Houghton Mifflin Company in Boston.

In a preface to the text Pyle discussed his students' illustrations: "I do not know whether the world will find an equivalent pleasure to my own in the pictures that illustrate this book, for there is a singular delight in beholding the lucid thoughts of a pupil growing into form and color; the teacher enjoys a singular pleasure in beholding his instruction growing into a definite shape. Nevertheless, I venture to think that the drawings possess both grace and beauty."[6]

In this work Smith clearly shows the Pyle influence. Yet only ten years before when her first published illustration appeared in the children's monthly magazine, *St. Nicholas,* one could readily recognize other influences. Her small illustration, which was accompanied by an original poem, showed "Five Little Maidens in a Row," who could just as easily have been drawn by Kate Greenaway or Maud Humphrey as by Smith. Greenaway's delicate line drawings with their simple images of toddlers in long dresses and bonnets came from England to delight American children. Humphrey, a graduate of the Art Students' League in New York and the Academie Julian in Paris, was the most prominent children's book illustrator in America in the 1880s. Her simple line drawings of wide-eyed youngsters in floor-length dresses were extremely popular. In her

9. Cover illustration for
Good Housekeeping,
June, 1925

early years as an illustrator, Smith attempted to emulate both Greenaway and Humphrey, a method that represented a logical key to entry into the world of the professional illustrator.

But what a transformation had come about after study with Pyle. The December, 1901, issue of *St. Nicholas* saw an indeed different illustration by Smith. No longer a simple line drawing of a squat little child, her "Little Puritan" illustration featured a historically costumed girl standing in a grove of trees. The child not only assumed a Puritan stance, but her face revealed all the adult seriousness that contributed to the demeanor of the Puritan child. But Smith was also wise enough to show more than one side of this life in her illustration. The stern portrait was carefully balanced by two panels showing Puritan children at play.

Smith was well aware of and grateful for Pyle's influence on her work. She once wrote, "At the Academy we had to think about compositions as an abstract thing, whether we needed a spot here or a break over here to balance, and there was nothing to get hold of. With Mr. Pyle it was absolutely changed. There was your story, and you knew your characters, and you imagined what they were doing, and in consequence you were bound to get the right composition because you lived these things . . . It was simply that he was always mentally projected into his subject."[7]

Pyle's enthusiastic student rarely directed her artistic sights beyond early romantic love stories or the later childhood images which were to become her speciality. In many ways her future was still being shaped by the mores of her time. After completing Pyle's courses at Drexel in 1897, Smith was offered a teaching post at the School of Design for Women. Her reply to the principal, Emily Sartain, was a regretful no. She admitted that she would have enjoyed teaching but thanks to Pyle's help in finding illustration commissions, she had already achieved some success and was beset with new assignments. But Smith also let her sex, or rather her image of woman's abilities, prevent her from attempting the extra workload.

"You have put your plea most temptingly and flatteringly in the face of what Howard Pyle is able to accomplish in his life," she wrote to Miss Sartain. "The excuse of being too busy is such a feeble one. However, he brings a man's strength and endeavour to it. I can duly judge for myself and realize that my woman's strength would be too severely taxed if I undertook a class in addition to all the rest."[8]

Possibly she was right. But if being a woman kept her from a teaching post, by the same token it contributed to her understanding, her love of children, and the immense humanity that shaped her work. She once remarked to her friend and artist colleague, Edith Emerson, that she enjoyed watching children "busy with their own affairs."[9] Anyone who sees a Smith illustration readily comprehends much of the pleasure she found in young children. Whether reading a storybook, playing in a sandbox, or gazing dreamily out to sea, her youngsters are immeasurably purposeful. For all their youth and innocence, there is a precocious sincerity about any of their activities. They transmit adult intensities to their child's play and their immense involvement in whatever they do touches everyone who has ever known or been a child.

But there is an even deeper side to her works. The scenes of motherly love which she so carefully painted are touching and delicate, yet in some ways undeniably sad. For we know that Smith remained a spinster all her life, but unlike Oakley who also lived a single life, she made mother's love an important touchstone in her art. It is a dominant theme that speaks volumes about her own needs and desires, and this is why her art is so deeply touching.

In writing about her work after her death, *The New York Times* noted, "The children that Miss Smith painted were reflective and a little sedate, and in her art the maternal note predominated. She seemed to be haunted by the vision of two faces, and the face of one was the face of a mother."[10]

One is tempted to draw parallels between Smith and Mary Cassatt, also known

for her portraits of mothers and children. Recognized as the only American artist invited to join the Impressionists in France, Cassatt is the more objective of the two women. Her mothers and children were not always the flawless, heaven-formed creatures created by Smith. But any mother who has dressed a small child for the snow or kissed a scratched finger will possibly disagree, for she will see something in Smith's mother/child portraits that she will not find in those of Cassatt.

10. Cover illustration for *Good Housekeeping,* July, 1930

These women both Philadelphians, both favoring similar themes never met, yet they shared an understanding of a kind of love neither had personally known, the love of a mother for her child. It is easy to speculate: had either of them had her own children would those marvelous energies have instead been, devoted to raising her own and would the art never have been put to canvas? Easy to speculate, but impossible to answer.

Some critics have noted that Smith was too sentimental. Her children are too innocent, too adorable to be real. Only a mother can verify or deny the truth of her images. Her popularity as an illustrator of over 35 children's books and scores of magazine covers is perhaps testament enough to her effectiveness and to the truth in her work. Her covers for *Good Housekeeping* magazine alone span nearly 15 years. Monthly images of children at play and of mother love are not continued out of habit. The magazine's management well understood the appeal her works held for millions of readers.

The children seen in the following pages of this book are the children that Smith wanted us to see. Dirty faces, naughty thoughts, and past sins were left to other illustrators to explore if they wished them. In her life and her art, it was the ideal that predominated, and the ideal child is the legacy left us by this remarkable artist.

1·Biography
Woman and Illustrator

ESSIE Willcox Smith was not a public person. She was almost reclusive in her relationship with her public. She kept no diaries, no journals, and almost inevitably she refused interviews and public appearances. A writer for the *Philadelphia Public Ledger* who secured an interview with Smith after repeated phone calls to her Cogshill home wrote that she was "firm in her antipathy to publicity of any kind."[11]

Most biographical portraits of Smith begin with her entry into Philadelphia's School of Design for Women, mentioning her early career as a kindergarten teacher only briefly. It is perhaps a fair way to begin the story of her career since she showed no inclination toward art as a child, had no artists in her family, and until age 18 had no idea that she could make her living as an illustrator.

Smith was born on September 3, 1863, the youngest girl in a family of two sisters and two brothers. Her father, Charles Henry Smith, was an investment broker originally from New York, who moved the family to Philadelphia before Jessie's birth to develop his growing investment business in that city. Her mother, Katherine DeWitt (Willcox) Smith, was originally from Connecticut.

The Smiths, being new to Philadelphia, and having no family ties in that area, did not make immediate entry into the locked doors of Philadelphia society. A listing in the Philadelphia Social Register was no easy prize for newcomers to obtain. Smith's parents were not wealthy, but her father did make a good living, and they eventually settled into a comfortable home at 210 South 41st Street.

Their youngest daughter was educated at private elementary schools in Philadelphia, and at 17 her parents sent her to join cousins who lived in Cincinatti to finish her schooling. It is not known why Smith had to travel so far to continue her studies. There were few, if any, artistic opportunities in that distant city, and Smith herself admitted that at the time "the margins of my schoolbooks were perfectly clean and unsullied with any virgin attempts at drawing."[12] She did, however, express an inclination to work with children and directed her first ambitions toward teaching, one of the few professions considered appropriate for a young woman at the time. Possibly there were more options available to Smith in education in Ohio. She continued her studies there, while living with her cousins, and within a year she obtained her first post as a kindergarten teacher.

Not long after embarking on her first career Smith complained that her height was a serious handicap. She felt that she was too tall to deal with children, bending down constantly to care for her demanding little students, suffering physically as a result. Whether this was an excuse for a suddenly discovered distinerest in her chosen profession cannot now be known. But we do know that Smith was elegantly tall and graceful. One admirer once para-phrased Virgil and remarked, "In her walk, the Goddess stood revealed."[13] She had long, black hair, which she wore demurely in a bun at the back or, in freer moments, tied loosely in a Victorian version of the pony tail. Smith preferred stately, simple clothes, even during her youth, and she is always pictured in floor length gowns, free of excessive decoration and jewelry.

She was not beautiful but there was an almost Oriental feeling to her deep-set eyes, as though she were hiding thoughts that would never be known to others. Smith was soft spoken and amazingly modest. Throughout her career, she never let vanity direct her actions or relationships with others. She knew when her work was successful, when it was not, and she was more inclined to openly talk of her failures than her successes. She never dominated a conversation, yet she always tried to offer something of importance. Her warmth and her human understanding were qualities recalled by both her lifelong friends and by those who modeled for her as children.

Smith's career as an artist began by chance, one could even say because of social conventions. She was asked to accompany a cousin who was planning to give drawing lessons to a young professor who wished help in illustrating his lectures on the blackboard in his classes. Smith recalled the first evening "art class", when she had taken up a pencil merely to keep company as best as possible. "We sat at a large center table on which a student lamp was burning and possibly because that was the most obvious thing in the room, our teacher suggested that we draw the lamp."[14] The young professor gave up his lessons after two days, but Smith, whose talent was recognized immediately, was advised by her friends to stop teaching kindergarten, "at which I may as well confess, I was not making a brilliant success – and go to art school."[15]

After corresponding with her parents and telling them about her dissatis-faction with her kindergarten career and her interest in art, they consented to her return to Philadelphia. She soon joined them in their 210 South 41st Street home.

In 1885 she enrolled in classes at the School of Design for Women, which was later named the Moore College of Art. While there she studied portrait painting with William Sartain, but his was one of the few classes which pleased her.

In the fall of that year, she transferred to the Pennsylvania Academy of the Fine Arts where she studied with, among others, the volatile Thomas Eakins. She did not hesitate in expressing her feelings about him. She thought he was a brilliant artist, but he was also a "madman," and she revealed that almost anything could happen during his classes.[16] Working in Eakins' classes was not an easy matter. One critic reported, "Only the most tenacious student could subject herself to the rigorous demands of Eakins' teaching, which made no allowances for the 'frailties' of women."[17] Certainly, he used conventional techniques. Almost a fanatic on anatomical studies, Eakins shifted the emphasis

11. Smith at age 25

12. Violet Oakley at work in the 1523 Chestnut Street studio which she shared with Smith and Elizabeth Shippen Green

from the drawing of antique casts to painting and modeling directly from the human figure. He also initiated the most intensive anatomical studies ever conducted at any art school, going so far as dissecting cadavers for his lessons in internal anatomy. He was eventually asked to leave the Academy for removing a loin cloth from a male model during a women's life class when he wanted to demonstrate the origin of a muscle, saying nudes could not be painted wearing a loin cloth. The Academy's angry officials were not ready for such dramatic demonstrations in 1886, and Eakins was obliged to leave. Smith never complained about his teaching methods, but she did once recall an incident in which an hysterical woman entered their anatomy class screaming that Eakins was her husband whom she had secretly married. The woman had to be forcibly evicted.[18] There was never a dull moment at the Academy while he was present.

Eakins, an accomplished photographer, was probably responsible for Smith's early interest in the camera as an aid to her illustrations. Early photographs of Academy students show them in togas and other ancient regalia posed for later transfer into drawn portraits. Unconventional and daring, Eakins was also a strong proponent of the rights of his female students to equal study opportunities at the Academy and during his time at that institution, the last elements of unequal training for men and women were abolished. After he lost his job at the Academy, he and his more loyal students organized the Philadelphia Art Students League. Smith was not a reformer. While she may have sympathised with the goals of the League, she continued her study at the Academy and absorbed whatever lessons were available.

Another important step in Smith's career occurred at the Academy. In 1888, at the 58th Annual Academy Exhibition, Smith's painting, "An Idle Moment," was number 313 in an exhibit of nearly 400 works. The painting is no longer recorded today, and the subject matter is therefore unknown, although the title makes one suspect the canvas could have included a child. This was the first public exhibit of a work by Smith and also the first of over 50 Academy exhibits in which she would participate during her lifetime.

In June of that year, Smith had completed her course of study at the Academy and began to search for work as an illustrator. Her first assignments were freelance and her first sale after graduation was to a firm called Dreka in Philadelphia, a notions manufacturer. One of the company's clients was having a dinner party before a performance of Gilbert and Sullivan's *The Mikado,* and Smith was commissioned to paint Japanese figures on the place cards. Her first illustration was also sold in that year and published in the May issue of *St. Nicholas Magazine.*

Smith was certainly aware of the many publications for children that had been circulated in the United States. Most were European imports, books like the *Kate Greenaway Almanacks,* begun in 1883 and continued until 1897, or Greenaway's popular *Marigold Garden,* and the numerous books of nursery rhymes and other poems designed for children during the period. In her days as a kindergarten teacher, Smith had been exposed to such works on a daily basis, and it is small wonder that she would not see her own potential for the field early in her art career.

She was living with her parents at the time, but longed for her own home and studio. Illustrations for children's magazines and for place cards did not bring in a large income, and in 1889 she applied to work at *The Ladies' Home Journal,* which was located in Philadelphia. She was accepted by the publication's advertising department, and her first job in the publishing world involved a variety of tasks: drawing line vignettes and borders which accompanied editorial matter, creating finished art from rough sketches submitted by contributors in the field, and preparing art for advertisers who relied on in-house artists to convey their messages. These last ranged from long underwear advertisements to soap. Though the work could not be called artistically broadening, it did give Smith a firm basis on which to begin her career as an illustrator. Her familiarity with the needs of publications, knowing what they could not publish due to artistic and mechanical restrictions, would be invaluable to her in her later career.

Aware of the high earnings received by outside illustrators who were working for *The Ladies' Home Journal* at the time, among them Charles Dana Gibson and Howard Chandler Christy, Smith was determined to grab the first opportunity

13. Violet Oakley's first cover for *Ladies' Home Journal,* November, 1897

for growth as an illustrator. That opportunity came in 1894 when Howard Pyle began teaching his class in illustration at Drexel Institute of Arts and Sciences. In his first year of teaching, classes met on Saturday afternoon at 2 P.M., a fortunate circumstance for Smith who worked from Monday to Friday. She applied for admission, taking the required drawing examination, passed and became one of the first 39 students in Pyle's class.

The experience changed her view of an illustrator's role almost immediately. She had always maintained an interest in painting portraits, perhaps in becoming a fine artist, and her experience at *The Ladies' Home Journal* certainly colored her view of the profession of illustration. Tight deadlines, hysterical art directors, great ideas slashed to pieces to satisfy the needs of a public – she saw them all at the Journal. When she joined Pyle's class, her view of the craft of illustration finally took on a different light. "When, however, I came under the guidance of Howard Pyle I began to think of illustration in a light different from that of a 'pot-boiler' "[19]

This wonderful partnership between teacher and student was an immediate success. Pyle readily recognized her talent and he assisted her from the first in finding herself through illustrations, encouraging her to select topics with which she felt comfortable. Pyle, happy to find commissions for Smith, provided her with one of her first major projects, a book of boy's stories of Indians. Smith, anxious to please her teacher, and eager for any publishing opportunities, accepted, asking the husband of a fellow student, Alice Barber Stephens, if she could study his collection of American Indian artifacts and costumes. He consented, of course, and she created the pictures successfully. So successfully, in fact, that Pyle was asked if this remarkable artist could supply more of the same for another book. Smith consented to do the project, but when the publisher requested a third, she called it all to a halt: "I felt I must speak or forever be condemned to paint Indians. So I wrote to the publisher that I did not know much about Indians and that if they had just an every-day book about children, I thought I could do it better. I was immediately rewarded with one of Louisa M. Alcott's stories, and a letter saying they were glad to know I did other things as they had supposed Indians were my speciality!"[20]

No published records indicate the names of the work containing the Indian pictures, but a 1900 edition of *The Head of the Hundred,* by Maud Wilder Goodwin, may be one of the works. Containing five illustrations, the story concerns our Pilgrim heritage and one of the plates shows fierce Indians in a forest, a broad departure from what one would expect from Smith, but again, a credit to her versatility. Since there is no other record of another Little, Brown published book which features Indians, it is conceivable that the second volume of illustrations was never published.

Part of the benefit of attending Pyle's class came from interacting with other students, young men and women who were interested in careers as illustrators, not as portrait painters or landscape artists. One of the other students who joined the afternoon and evening class was Elizabeth Shippen Green, a good natured young woman who had heard about Pyle's teaching while she studied at the Academy. Coincidentally, Green had obtained a position in the advertising

14. Illustration for the
Bryn Mawr College
Calendar, 1902

department at *The Ladies' Home Journal,* after she illustrated catalogs for the
Strawbridge and Clothier department store. Possibly she obtained her Journal
post after meeting and making friends with Smith, who may have introduced
her at the magazine.

In physical appearance, Green was the antithesis of her friend. Short, with an
inclination to plumpness, she had a smiling, round face and an active, outgoing
personality. She was always the first to make a joke, the first to suggest a party
or informal gathering when the opportunity was ripe. Yet lest her good nature
belie her serious attitudes toward her work, let it be said that her output proves
that her artistic intentions were immensely serious.

Another early Pyle student was Hester Oakley, sister of Violet Oakley. The latter was studying at the Academy in 1896 while the others were with Pyle at Drexel. Hester urged her sister to transfer to Pyle's classes, and in 1897 she joined the other women at Drexel. This was the beginning of a life-long friendship and it was also one of the most important illustrator partnerships the country had ever seen. Almost immediately, Pyle recognized the similarities in the work of Smith and Oakley, both of whom had strong decorative inclinations, and he teamed them for their first major illustrative work, Henry Wadsworth Longfellow's *Evangeline*. The first assignment proved to be something of a problem for the two women. Their respective homes in Philadelphia were a good distance away from each other, and they could only consult on the work while they were in class, a situation that was serviceable though inconvenient.

The year prior to their meeting, Smith left her parent's home and moved to a small studio at 1334 Chestnut Street, the building where artists Stephen Parrish and Cecilia Beaux also had studios at one time. She was located in the center of downtown Philadelphia and within walking distance of her *Ladies' Home Journal* job, but her studio was modest and space was a serious problem.

Smith and Oakley decided to move together to another studio location. They were joined by Jessie H. Dowd, another Pyle student, and the women found a perfect three room studio-cum-living quarters at 1523 Chestnut Street, owned by Mr. Clement C. Love. The new tenants affectionately called him Clemency Love because his rental of $18 monthly per person was fair enough for three struggling young artists.

16. "A Game of Ball" ink and wash, 1903.

Compared to her previous work area, the new location was resplendent with space. An early photo of young Oakley in the studio shows how it was a comfortable hodge-podge of chintz, oriental rugs, patterned pillows, drawings, sculptures, and other recent creations by its artist inhabitants. At a later date, the trio was joined briefly by Ellen W. Ahrens who made a temporary move to this inner-city artist's colony, and they were later joined by Elizabeth Shippen Green. Green had recently returned from a tour of England, France, and Belgium. Accompanied by her mother, she had gone there to visit the museums, and she returned with a wealth of sketches and experiences to share with the other artists.

In the new studios, the women's various tastes combined to create a wonderfully eclectic atmosphere. Early photographs reveal a great deal about the inhabitants. A print of the *Mona Lisa* by DaVinci shared space on the same wall with an 1897 *Harper's Magazine* poster by Edward Penfield. In Oakley's study corner, she proudly displayed a Thanksgiving design which was her first cover for *The Ladies' Home Journal,* while four decorative panneaux by the Belgian poster artist Privat-Livemont hung only a few feet away. Quaint, cluttered, and heavily charged with the electrical energy of creation, this first studio set the stage for the further growth and development of Smith, Green, and Oakley as important American illustrators.

It is not surprising that so diverse a selection of artworks should appear in the women's studio. Since illustration was their business, they were aware of all new trends in the field, and it is safe to presume that these influences did find their way into their works. Smith's admiration for Edward Penfield may have encouraged her to emulate the Japanese simplicity which dominates his works. A great connoisseur of the Japanese print which had become popular in France and the United States in the late 1800s, Penfield's monthly *Harper's* posters were seen in almost every bookseller's window. Each month a new design appeared to intrigue and delight Smith and her friends.

Another artist whose works were predominant in Philadelphia at the time and who had a major, obvious influence on Smith was Boutet de Monvel, the French poster designer and children's book illustrator. One of Smith's early drawings, "A Game of Ball," shows two children throwing a ball in a room which is richly decorated with flowered wallpaper and a patterned floor. The children wear checked nightgowns. The picture is static in its composition; though the boy and girl are playing an active game, they look frozen. This was an important feature of de Monvel's illustrations, as was the extensive use of pattern and decoration. As if to publicly exclaim his influence on the picture, Smith drew a copy of his famous poster, "Petite Poucette," into the background. When the picture was exhibited at the Plastic Club, a Philadelphia arts organization, in an 1898 show, it was described as "a small gem" by one of the reviewing critics.[21]

In January of that year Oakley and Smith had exhibited their original illustrations for *Evangeline* at the Academy Annual, where the works met with a favourable reception, indeed remarkable in the Academy climate where illustrations were not always viewed with the greatest favor.

By this time the women were confident enough to devote their full energies to illustration, and Smith and Green left their jobs at *The Ladies' Home Journal*. With Howard Pyle's help, the women continued to develop their contacts in the publishing world. Green continued to illustrate articles for the Journal on a free-lance basis, but she added to her credentials work for *The Saturday Evening Post* and *Forward* the illustrated young people's weekly. Oakley, setting aside illustration for a while, obtained an important commission which would occupy her for the next two years: a group of murals, altar decorations and stained glass windows for the All Angels Church in New York. Smith also obtained new projects, among them two books of pictures illustrating Nathaniel Hawthorne's works for Houghton Mifflin, and two books for Little, Brown and Company, *Brenda, Her School and Her Club* and *Brenda's Summer at Rockley,* both by Helen Leah Reed. While these subjects did not exactly reach the high standards of literature that Smith could have hoped for, she was coming gradually closer to the books about children which were to become a staple of her career.

Changes in the women's lifestyles were happening rapidly. In the autumn of 1899 Jessie H. Dowd, who had become a close friend and confidant of Smith, announced that she would have to return to her home in Ohio. Dowd suffered from painful headaches, some of which lasted entire days, and the pressures of her illustrator's life, which was not as successful as that of her friends, were too much for her to bear. It was a sad day for all the women when she departed. Their gift to her was a Friendship Calendar for the year 1900. Stacked neatly and tied with green ribbon, the calendar featured a page for each day of the coming year, on which one of her friends had drawn an amusing illustration, quoted from a literary work, or written a personal message. Some of the messages written to Dowd by Smith give great insight into Smith's personal viewpoints. On July 18 she wrote "After all, say what we will, the one supreme luxury of life is sympathetic companionship." September 24 read "The fine art of living, indeed, is to draw from each person his best."[22]

By the following summer, Smith, Green, and Oakley, who already had more than enough work to fill the summer months, began to search for a more comfortable place to live and work. They all realized how much better they would work in the country, free from the noise and preoccupations of city life. The dream of a country studio began to form in each woman's mind. Packing their belongings, they traveled to Bryn Mawr, not far from Philadelphia by today's standards, but far enough at the turn of the century to warrant their renting a summer residence where they could work in peace.

One of the places high on their list of possible homes was the Red Rose Inn near Villa Nova, near Bryn Mawr. Located on the estate of Moro Phillips, a wealthy philanthropist, the inn was the crown jewel in an estate of over 800 acres, Stoke Pogis. Situated one an one-half miles from the Villa Nova train station, the inn was modeled after a typical Tudor road tavern, with low rambling buildings, a lake, and terraced gardens. At one time, it was Phillips' own home, but he later leased it to parties who used it as an inn. The three women stayed at the inn during the summer of 1900, falling in love with the simply furnished house, the terraced lawns, and the beautiful trees. It was an otherwordly

17. A 1921 portrait of Huger Elliott by Violet Oakley

atmosphere which inspired their creativity and happiness. Oakley luxuriated contently in the transcendental feeling of the estate. Taking daily strolls across the grounds, she recited poetry as she walked, saying once that a nearby meadow was "four Sonnets from the Portuguese away from the house."[23]

The original stone building was a farmhouse which dated back to 1787. In 1893, it had been remodeled for use as an inn. A formal garden was added, the lawn was terraced, and hedges were planted which separated the garden, the quadrangle, and an outer and inner courtyard. Among its more romantic features were a gazebo, a thick-walled stone spring house, and two high story outbuildings, which the women used as their studios. On their way to work each morning, they passed a large grape arbor, and an empty, abandoned green-house. It was a perfect setting for every dream the women ever had. They had heard rumors near the end of that first summer that the property was for sale. Oakley, never one to be afraid to ask, inquired of the owners if the rumors were true. The property was indeed available, but only if the buyer purchased the entire acreage, making the price impossible for even the combined incomes of all three women.

Despondent over the property's being on the market and the uncertain fate of their summer retreat, the women returned to their city studio, frustrated by the lack of space and wondering how they could now continue to work in such cramped conditions after the freedom of the country.

Early in 1901 word arrived that the Phillips estate had been sold, to one Anthony J. Drexel. No sooner had the announcement appeared in the news-papers than the women approached him about leasing the Red Rose Inn for their needs. Drexel, delighted at the prospect of having such distinguished illustrators living on his property, consented, and on May 1, 1901 Smith, Green, and Oakley began their first one year lease on the Inn and the adjacent studio buildings.

Oakley said, after the arrangements had been finalized, "This is not going to be an artist's colony at all. We have grown tired of working in the midst of trolley cars, drays, and all the noise of heavy traffic, so we three are going out where green trees grow, where the cows roam and where the air is pure, and quietness prevails."[24]

The Red Rose Inn, however, saw more than three new occupants that spring. Along with Oakley came her ailing mother, while Green brought both parents to join her. There is no record of Smith's parents coming to live with the trio at the inn, nor are there any published announcements of their subsequent deaths or departure from the Philadelphia area. Possibly both her parents died while she was at work for the Journal or during her time of study with Pyle. They may also have moved from the area or simply made no intrusions into their daughter's adult life.

Another addition to the Red Rose household was Henrietta Cozens, a young woman who had befriended Green at an earlier date, and who came to her artist friend in time of need. She had been living in the Adirondack Mountains, while caring for an invalid brother. After his death, her sole function taken from her, she turned to Green in her grief and confusion. The artist invited her to join the family at the inn, and Cozens became a permanent resident. The small, wiry young woman was very serious and determined to contribute her share to the household. Though she had no artistic talent and could not make a living as an illustrator, she was excellent at managing funds and performing the daily necessities of operating a household of this magnitude. The image of Cozens, always dressed in long gowns, wearing her customary silver chains, and over-seeing tradesmen, was a common one at the Red Rose Inn. Never having had much money herself, she had the ability to make each cent count, and her management of the household affairs freed the other women from concerns that could only interfere with their art.

Because she was so petite, Cozens often posed for her friends when they wanted a "little girl" model on short notice, but it was Cozen's talent as a gardener that most endeared her to the others. Her knowledge of plant life was formidable, and all the women were grateful for such lovely gardens to use as backgrounds in their pictures. In later years, when Cozens recreated the Red Rose Inn gardens at Cogslea, their next residence, Oakley and Smith presented her with a book called *The Lure of the Garden*. On the title page they wrote, "To the Alluring Gardner from her sisters who say, 'how lovely,' and sit in the shade."[25]

The gardens were also a fine playground for the ever-present cats that lived at the inn. In a cleverly stretched hammock or in a lawn chair overlooking the nearby meadow, Smith would often sit quietly with one of the cats in her lap, silently contemplating the view, taking well-deserved respite from her work. She had a special affinity for cats, especially the long-haired Persian variety. Like herself, they were quiet, graceful, and something of an enigma. Throughout her life, Smith had her silent feline companions, Midget, Cogs, and others.

Days at the Red Rose Inn were relaxed but never lazy. Each woman had established herself firmly in her chosen profession, and each was busy earning enough to pay her fair share in the upkeep of the household. In August, 1901 Green signed a long term contract with *Harper's* which would renew itself until 1924. Smith was devoting more of her time to book and magazine illustration than ever before, actually having trouble keeping up with her many new assignments. These early days at the inn were truly the most idyllic that any of the women had yet experienced.

Early in 1902 Oakley, after successfully completing the All Angels Church commission, received an important assignment to decorate the Governor's Reception Room at the new Pennsylvania State Capitol building in Harrisburg. In the autumn of that year she and her mother left for a six-month study tour of Europe to prepare for this formidable task.

Smith achieved national attention that same year when she was awarded the bronze medal for paintings exhibited at the International Charleston, South Carolina Exposition. Smith entered her works in many such competitions. Like any good business woman, she understood that official recognition meant more public attention, and that led of course to more illustration assignments from editors who wished to please their reading publics. World expositions were a popular feature of the early twentieth century, and they were likewise an important means of communication, where citizens could see first-hand the very latest developments in industry and art.

Another important vehicle for the work of Smith and Green was the 1902 Bryn Mawr College Calendar which they illustrated at the request of the college. The two-tone drawings feature young women on horseback in a forest, traveling in Europe, or working on their lessons.

This successful collaboration inspired the women to team again on "The Child," a self-invested calendar project that featured some of the most beautiful works either woman ever painted. In touching, sensitive artistic statements, they immortalized young toddlers who gardened, warmed their feet before a fire, or played at motherhood. In almost no time, Stokes, a New York publishing

18. A 1916 Christmas Greeting sent from Cogshill by Smith

Christmas Greeting
Cogskill
1916

Jessie Willcox Smith

19. Portrait of Henrietta
Cozens by Violet
Oakley, posed against
the gardens of Cogslea,
c. 1930

house, asked to reprint the work as a book. Mabel Humphrey, one of the most popular children's authors of the day was commissioned to write a series of poems to match the pictures, and within a few months, *The Book of the Child* was made available to a receptive public. More than any other work, this creation brought Smith and Green into the limelight. Neither woman would ever have to worry again about lack of illustrative assignments.

More formal recognition of Smith came in 1903, when the Academy awarded its prestigious Mary Smith prize to the quickly advancing alumnus. The prize, established at the Academy in 1879, was given each year "to the painter of the best painting (not excluding portraits) in oil or watercolors exhibited at the Academy, painted by a resident woman artist for qualities ranking as follows:

1st, Originality of Subject; 2ND, Beauty of Design or Drawing; 3RD, Color and Effect, and lastly, Execution."[26] The namesake of the prize was the daughter of painter Russell Smith, who was concerned over lack of encouragement for women artists in Philadelphia. Certainly the $100 award was insignificant by Smith's standards of earning, but the prestige was unquestionably important to her.

Prizes were a big subject of conversation at the Red Rose Inn in 1904. Violet Oakley won the Gold Medal for illustration at the St. Louis International Exposition, and Smith followed close on her heels with a Silver Medal. Oakley also won the Silver Medal for mural decoration at the same exposition, this one for her All Angels Church commission. One could well imagine the jubilation at the Red Rose Inn when those awards were announced.

The happy life the women had made for themselves at the Red Rose Inn changed dramatically in 1905 when two events of importance occurred: Elizabeth Shippen Green met and became engaged to Huger Elliott, a young Philadelphia architect; and Anthony Drexel sold the Red Rose Inn.

The first of these events was bittersweet. All the women had come to enjoy Elliott's company, his sharp wit and congenial conversation at their afternoon teas. But with her eventual marriage to him would also come Green's departure from the household, an event that would cause sadness. Elliott had been introduced to the artists at the Red Rose Inn by Mr. and Mrs. George Woodward, wealthy neighbors from Chestnut Hill who had been friends of Green's mother and father. Green was 34 when she met her suitor; she had long since given up any thoughts of marriage and had instead devoted herself to her career. But Elliott was persistent, determined to marry her at once. The two were plainly in love, but Green made one stipulation on accepting the engagement: they would not marry until after the death of her parents. She had supported them for some time now; both were seriously ill, and frankly she was unwilling to burden her future husband with their responsibility. She was firm in this decision and did not become Mrs. Elliott until 1911, six years later, when she was 40 years old.

The other event that made 1905 such an important year for the women was less pleasant, one that caused both emotional and legal stress. On August 27, the Red Rose Inn and its estate was sold to H. S. Kerbaugh, a Philadelphia contractor who had no interest in the reputations of the young artists or in their rental income. Saying he did not want any "beggarly" artists living on his property, he refused to renew their lease and attempted to have them evicted. One could well imagine the stormy events that transpired when the county sheriff, arriving at the inn to "read them out," came face to face with an angry Oakley and Cozens.[27]

It was a major crisis and the women invited their friends, the Woodwards, to tea to explain the dilemma. They had families to care for, they needed work space, and they had to have the peace of the country. None of them could ever return to a city studio. The Woodwards, sympathetic to their plight, offered them some of their own property, Hill Farm, in nearby Chestnut Hill. The site was a handsome piece of land which could easily adapt to the needs of the women. Located below a steep slope which led to the Wissahickon Creek, the

property included a farmhouse, a barn, a carriage house, and a nearby mill. The Woodwards, who enjoyed their role as American Medicis, refurbished the carriage house into studios and modernized the farmhouse into their living quarters, all at a rental within the budgets of the artists.

The carriage house made a perfect studio. Long and wide, nearly three fourth's of its area was allocated to Oakley, whose murals took up great space, and who desperately needed room in which to work. Smith and Green converted the remaining area into one studio which they shared. Henrietta Cozens almost immediately went to work recreating the gardens from the Red Rose Inn at the new home. Within a short time, the women artists had exterior settings as colorful and fragrant as those they had left.

At one of the daily afternoon teas, when all the residents converged in the front parlor, they debated over the name of their new home. Cozens, Oakley, Green, and Smith, using the first initials of their last names, came up with COGS, which was quickly finalized as Cogslea. The name Cogs was instead reserved for a household pet, a newly-arrived kitten.

As the new residents settled into the Cogslea atmosphere, the household began to grow. Cozens was able to hire a large staff of servants, including a cook, two maids, and a helper in the garden. Smith's brother, Dewitt, who had

21. A view of Cogshill drawn by Huger Elliott for Smith's 1922 Christmas card

COGSHILL
CHRISTMAS — 1922

Greetings from HENRIETTA COZENS & JESSIE WILLCOX SMITH

been suffering from a prolonged illness, was finally invited to move in with her where he could have constant attention. At a later date, an elderly aunt also would join Smith's household.

Smith's generosity was boundless. Her income was of course very healthy, especially late in her career, and at one time she was responsible for the financial support of 11 children. A severe debilitating illness resulted in her sister's inability to properly support her children, and at one point, Smith assumed their financial responsibility. When one of her cousins died, leaving her children as orphans, another relative offered to house them if Smith would pay their keep. She did so without question for several years. Her large earnings encouraged her friends to call her "The Mint", a term that affectionately characterized her generosity.[28]

The early Cogslea years were peaceful and happy. In 1905, Oakley became the second woman after Cecelia Beaux to win the Gold Medal of Honor from the Pennsylvania Academy, just cause for certain celebration among Cogslea's residents. In 1907, Smith, Green, and Oakley exhibited their works at a Society of Illustrators Exhibit at the Waldorf Astoria Hotel in New York with those of two other women illustrators, Florence Scovel Shinn and May Wilson.

Life at Cogslea was peaceful, yet active. Smith had a regular parade of youngsters in and out of her studios, so the blossom of youth kept the grounds vibrant with children's laughter and happy faces. Oakley had become deeply committed to Christian Science, and she was devoting more of her time to religious affairs.

Smith was not actively religious, although she had accepted the Swedenborgian faith. She had been influenced by Howard Pyle who had himself developed an intense interest in the doctrines of Emanuel Swedenborg a Swedish scientist and theologian whose religious system had begun to gain popularity in the United States. The Swedenborgian "New Church" was located in center city Philadelphia, and Smith rarely mustered the energy to attend services there. She instead worshipped at an Episcopal Church in Chestnut Hill, giving annual contributions to both it and the "New Church".

While church services did not attract Smith into the city, such was not the case when it came to the opera and theatre. The women made regular pilgrimages into the city for those diversions, walking over a mile to the local train station for the transport into town. Walking was one of their favorite activities. Smith would walk briskly alone through the nearby countryside, making it her chief exercise and spiritual respite. In other times of relaxation, she enjoyed reading, especially the works of Henry James, and one could almost sense the mysterious, Jamesian atmosphere of the household of women and their families.

Cozens was fondly devoted to her gardens, but she also directed the social gatherings, the daily teas and the special events. On July 4TH, the women, all of whom were fervently patriotic, reaffirmed their faith in the American way. After a special celebratory dinner, Cozens would give a reading of the Declaration of Independence as each woman listened intently. After the reading, the women rose and signed the reprinted document between the names of the founders of our nation.[29]

Major events came to pass in 1911. By this time each woman was well established in her respective career. Smith had illustrated *Dream Blocks, A Child's Book of Old Verses, A Child's Book of Stories,* and other works which made her the most popular children's book illustrator of the day. Demand for her work was intense, and she was working without a free moment. Oakley, after the death of Edwin Austin Abbey, who had been commissioned to decorate the Senate chambers of the Pennsylvania state capitol, was quickly called in to complete the work, a project that demanded her full attention. Green was preoccupied with a full work schedule and her parents, both of whom died after separate illnesses in the same year.

Another death occurred in 1911 that shocked and saddened the Cogslea women. Howard Pyle, on a visit to Italy, died while overseas. His vitality and temperament had made it seem that he was possibly immortal, and in their grief, the women realized that Pyle's teachings were the only thing that would live forever, as long as there were students who produced work that reflected his greatness.

It was also the year of another important award for Smith, the Philadelphia Water Color Club's Beck Prize, given for the best work seen in its annual exhibit at the galleries at the Academy which had previously been reproduced in color in printed form. She won the award for "A Child's Grace," which showed a boy and girl at a table before a bowl of porridge, their heads bowed and hands clasped. Smith's works were also seen in the American pavillion at the Rome Exposition in 1911, and, reportedly, the Dowager Queen of Italy singled out her painting, "The Dark," expressing great delight on seeing it.

At Cogslea other news was developing. Finding the need for more space and privacy, and having the necessary income to support that goal, Smith approached the Woodwards about buying part of the property adjacent to Cogslea, where she could build a home and studio for herself. The Woodwards, who were disinclined to break up their large property holdings, but less inclined to lose Smith to another area of Philadelphia, consented to sell her one acre. It was a perfect spot for a house, just above Cogslea on the crest of the hill. Hiring an architect, Smith had him design a 16-room home which duplicated many of the features of the Red Rose Inn. The house was finally constructed between 1913 and 1914, but much of the building material, which had been ordered from Europe, was delayed because of the outbreak of war on the continent. When the home was finally finished, Smith moved in with her friend, Cozens, her brother, and an aunt, Mrs. Roswell Weston. They named the place, appropriately, Cogshill.

While Smith was contemplating her move, Green acted on her promise to Huger Elliott and she became his bride, moving with him to Rhode Island, where he accepted a post as director of the Rhode Island School of Design.

In 1913, Oakley began teaching a class in mural decoration at the Academy. One of her most promising students, Edith Emerson, worked closely with her at the Cogslea studio, preparing for her own future mural commissions, and she was eventually invited by Oakley to move into the home. She joined the household in 1913, helping to fill the void left by Green's departure, and contributing to the financial subsistence of the place.

Smith had in the meantime settled comfortably into her new home, continuing her work in a spacious new studio that faced one of Cozen's magnificently flowered gardens. In 1915 she received another important award, the water-color medal at the Panama/Pacific Exposition in San Francisco. Smith had also achieved a great personal satisfaction in that year, completing her series of illustrations for Charles Kingsley's *Water Babies,* which would be published the following year. As she expected, the book was a large success, and with that came dozens of offers from other publishers. Among the offers was a contract for covers for *Good Housekeeping Magazine.* She accepted it, and the first of these appeared in the December, 1917 issue, establishing a tradition at the publication that would continue through 1932.

Smith settled into a comfortable routine in her life at Cogshill, keeping up with her various book and magazine projects, and somehow managing to paint a number of children's portraits annually. Spinsterhood never seemed to trouble her, and she rarely spoke with regret about not having married. She was not without suitors in her youth, and in her middle years. At Cogshill she annually hosted a Swiss businessman who came to the United States once each year. Annually he made a proposal of marriage, and annually she would refuse.

When work pressures began to impose on her peaceful state of mind, she made a brief pilgrimage to Canada where a niece had a quiet home away from dead-lines and portrait commissions. Much of her time was devoted to portrait paint-ing during the early 1920s, and she maintained her close alliance with Oakley and Green, although the latter was more of a correspondence relationship since she had moved away from Philadelphia.

In December, 1923, the women briefly joined together again to participate in a memorial exhibition of Pyle students' works at the Public Library in Wilming-ton, Delaware.

Smith never accepted students, but she was available to advise and assist young illustrators. Carolyn Haywood, a friend of Smith, who is now herself the author and illustrator of numerous books for children, reported that while she was an art student, she visited her friend and learned that Postum cereal had asked Smith to design a new advertisement for them. In the best Howard Pyle tradi-tion, Smith wrote to the manufacturer and said she was unable to do the job but suggested Carolyn Haywood as an artist who could handle it just as well. Trust-ing her judgement, the company gave the commission to Haywood.

On occasion, Smith would visit with students at the Art School at Broad and Pine Street (now the Philadelphia College of Art) for a class criticism on com-position, although she was never on the faculty. James Kirk Merrick, who was an art student there in 1925, notes, "She was an inspiration to all of us. Her criticisms were keen, severe (never cruel) and always constructive."[30] He related a story of a dinner at the Philadelphia Art Alliance, followed by a performance of skater Sonia Henji and her troupe in her first touring ice show:

22. A watercolor portrait of Smith in the doorway to her Cogshill studio by Violet Oakley, c. 1930

The dinner was an occasion for all of us – dining at the Art Alliance among all the established artists of the area, *and* with Miss Smith as our hostess. The

ice show was at the Arena, an old beat-up boxing and wrestling place with wooden planks for seats, bleacher style – all unreserved. Jessie, followed by her young flock, hiked up her skirts and ran nimbly to find places, hopping from board to board like a mountain goat. She cheered and applauded like the rest of the crowd throughout the performance. . . . I saw her frequently until her death, and her vital youthful spirit always amazed and delighted me.[31]

In summer, 1927, Oakley left for a three-year trip to Europe, where she painted portraits of participants in the League of Nations meetings. She returned with volumes of sketches, as well as raves about European sights and events. Smith, who had never had a great desire for travel overseas, agreed with her friend that it was indeed now or never. In recent months, she had begun to have problems with her eyesight, a condition that led to near blindness just before her death.

By the time of her first trip to Europe in 1933, accompanied by a nurse and Isabel Lewis, Henrietta Cozen's neice, Smith was already suffering from various ailments. She had difficulty seeing and walking. It was thought that the European trip would have been relaxing, but instead it was another struggle for the now ailing artist. The trip took the voyagers to Naples, Palermo, Venice, Lisbon, and other warm European climates. When Smith returned to Cogshill her condition had deteriorated markedly, and on May 3, 1935, at age 72, she died in her sleep. The cause of death, as listed on the medical report was arteriosclerosis, interstital nephritis, and myocarditis. She was buried at Philadelphia's Woodland Cemetery.

Possibly one of the most fascinating Smith-related stories concerned Edith Emerson, who with Oakley awaited word about their friend's condition. The night of May 3, she dreamed that Smith, ill and bedridden, got out of her bed and dressed, despite her nurse's vigorous objections and attempts to keep her in bed. Smith said she wanted to go into the garden, and defiantly she opened the French windows leading to the gardens from her bedroom, turned, gave Emerson a mischievous smile, and hurried out into the night. Emerson awoke suddenly, knowing that Smith had died, and an hour later she received the call confirming the news.

In 1936, the Pennsylvania Academy of the Fine Arts sponsored a memorial exhibit of Smith's works, a gathering of over 100 items. In the Introduction to the catalog, Emerson paid tribute to her friend, offering a personal remembrance that sums up Jessie Willcox Smith with the sensitivity and understanding of one who knew her well:

Nothing morbid or bitter ever came from her brush. This is not because the difficulties of life left her untouched. She had more than her full share, but when they came she met and conquered them. She demanded nothing for herself but obeyed the simple injunction on the poster she designed for the Welfare Federation – *give*. She helped those in need, the aged, the helpless, the unfortunate. She gave honest and constructive advice to students who came to her for criticisms. She rejoiced in the success of others and was

23. Smith at work on a
portrait in her studio,
c. 1930

modest about her own. Tall, handsome and straightforward, she carried
herself well, with no trace of self-assertion. She always spoke directly and
to the point. She lived quietly and loved natural unaffected things and
people. Altogether, hers was a brave and generous mind, comprehending
life with a large simplicity, free from all pettiness, and unfailingly kind.[32]

2·The Howard Pyle Legacy

The Brandywine Women

NO discussion of Jessie Willcox Smith would be complete without due credit to that cornerstone of American illustration and her primary influence, Howard Pyle. The illustrators whose careers were altered or launched by his teachings are numerous. In addition to the Cogslea women, Pyle's students included Maxfield Parrish, N. C. Wyeth, Frank Schoonover, Alice Barber Stephens, Thornton Oakley and others – a veritable Who's Who of American illustrators.

Pyle's practical experience as an illustrator, his excellent taste, and his dedication to his craft combined with his powerful personality to leave the strongest, most visible mark of any art teacher in American history. His wisdom, frankness, and devotion to his students were the special tools with which he shaped the future of American illustration.

Smith readily admitted that after years of study at the School of Design for Women and the Academy, it was Pyle who "seemed to wipe away all the cobwebs and confusions that so beset the path of the art student."[33] The late Henry Pitz, illustrator and author, in his definitive volume on Pyle and his work, dubbed him "a missionary of Americanism," a man whose creative sense and richly inventive art are representative of the American ideal.[34]

Born in 1853 in Wilmington, Delaware, Pyle showed artistic talent as a child and received encouragement from his parents. They enrolled him in a private art school in Philadelphia under the direction of the Belgian artist, Van der Wielen. He stayed under his tutelage for several years before submitting and selling his first illustration and story to Scribner's Magazine in 1876.

Migrating to New York City the next year, he began his illustrative and writing career, submitting works to *Harper's Weekly, St. Nicholas*, and other publications. His talent obvious to his editors, the young man advanced quickly from magazine work to books, which he both wrote and illustrated. Among his more popular titles were *The Merry Adventures of Robin Hood, The Wonder Clock,* and *The Story of King Arthur and his Knights*.

The artist returned to Wilmington in 1879, where he married and began to raise a considerable family of seven children. Oddly enough, although he is best known as a teacher, Pyle did not consider teaching until he was 41 years old. Realizing that there was a dearth of qualified instructors available to those who wished to make a career of illustration, Pyle approached the Pennsylvania

24. Ethel Franklin Betts
Bains, illustration for
The Raggedy Man by
James Whitcomb Riley,
1907

Academy of the Fine Arts and proposed a course in illustration. He was flatly
rejected. The Academy deans claimed they were only interested in the "fine arts,"
and illustration was therefore not in the Academy's province. Pyle was justifiably
angered at the rejection, because he considered good illustration as much of an
art as portrait painting or mural work. He would be indeed disappointed to see
that today the snobbery of "art" vs. illustration has yet to be altered.

Pyle's rejection by the Academy did not end the man's teaching aspirations.
While he had made his suggestion to the Academy, more advanced administra-
tors at Philadelphia's Drexel Institute of the Arts and Sciences had already con-
ceived of a course in illustration, and Pyle was invited to teach there for one day
per week. In October, 1894, the first class of 39 people – a class that included
Jessie Willcox Smith – met for its first Saturday session with Pyle.

The class featured Pyle's illustrated lectures, and his students were given the rudiments of composition, practical illustration and technique, drawing from the costumed model, the elaboration of groups, and illustrative treatment of historical and other picturesque subjects. All student work was personally evaluated and critiqued by Pyle. The class was admittedly too large, and Pyle was frustrated at times by students whose ambitions did not live up to the positive predictions of their illustrated entrance exams. "I can't stand those damned women in the front row who placidly knit while I try to strike sparks from an imagination they don't have," wrote an angry Pyle about his less serious students.[35] No one has ever established who these women were, but one can be certain their names were not Smith, Green, or Oakley.

During the 1896/97 school year, Drexel expanded Pyle's program into a school of illustration, which included two full days of teaching on Monday and Friday. Then in 1898, with the cooperation of Drexel, Pyle established a special summer program of illustration studies at an old farm in Chadds Ford, Pennsylvania. This was the Brandywine region, where the meandering Brandywine River created a picturesque tableau of farmlands and natural beauties. Renting a large home for himself and his family, Pyle converted a nearby grist mill into a convenient studio and classroom. Scholarships of $100 each, supplied by Drexel, helped pay for student lodgings with nearby families.

By this time Smith, Green, and Oakley were well into their respective careers, and there is no record of their participation in the Chadds Ford classes. But for the students who did attend, it was an ideal atmosphere in which to benefit from Pyle's teaching. Pyle was well aware of the limited attention an artist received in formal art schools. Posed models grew tired after hours of keeping the same position, and this exhaustion could be seen clearly in the resulting works. Studio light was consistently monotonous, coming from the north, and artificially free of shadows. Pyle therefore took his students outdoors to the river banks, and into the forests along the colorful country byways. It was the perfect atmosphere for Pyle the teacher and for the eager young students to learn his craft.

Here they would illustrate subjects seen through the variegated patterns of light coming through the trees, or in the soft glow of sunset, or the bright dominant light of high noon. Sometimes he would ask them to sketch subjects seen in a semi-darkened room lit by only one candle. It was daring, it was different, but it reflected reality, and his students were all the more grateful as a result. His dynamism and alternative view of art could not help but reflect itself in his students' work. "If an object in the foreground of your picture looks too big," he once said, "make it bigger. If it is too small, make it smaller."[36]

Always daring, always willing to explore and experiment, he stimulated in his students a vision that would last for decades. N. C. Wyeth, in a perceptive introduction to Charles Abbott's biography of Pyle, wrote, "Howard Pyle's extraordinary ability as a teacher lay primarily in his penetration. He could reach beneath the crude lines on paper the true purpose and detect therein our real inclinations and impulses; in short, unlock our personalities."[37]

Pyle's lessons were not easily forgotten by his best students, and his influence was at times overpowering. Imitation, in fact, was one of the greatest dangers of studying with the Master. When *The Lamp* magazine interviewed Smith for an article about life at the Red Rose Inn, the interviewer questioned her about Pyle's teachings. She wrote, ". . . and Miss Smith declares that, under the strong propulsion of his teaching, it was impossible not to imitate him for a time, adding that his classes were filled with rows of temporary Howard Pyles in miniature."[38]

But Pyle expected more than mere imitation from his students: "I shall make it a requisite that the pupil whom I choose shall possess – first of all, imagination; secondly, artistic ability; thirdly, color and drawing; and I shall probably not accept any who are deficient in any of these three requisites. It is needless for me to say that my opinions as to the requisites of color and form may not be the same as those entertained by the art schools."[39]

Lessons already learned, therefore, often had to be cast aside and re-examined from Pyle's point of view. For example, one aspect of his teaching concerned costumes and accuracy of settings. An expert in costume history, he collected authentic clothes of several eras and types. Smith, who heeded his advice on this count, was herself an active collector of children's costumes.

Pyle's advice, however, was not always followed with blind enthusiasm by his students. He was never known to have worked from photographs and was suspicious about the artists who had to rely on the camera for visual accuracy. Smith, on the other hand, found the camera a valuable tool, and she made use of it for both her illustrative and portrait assignments.

Howard Pyle's greatest contribution to his young students, however, did not relate directly to the creation of images on the illustration board. In his years as a professional illustrator, he developed important contacts with publishers in the major publishing centers along the Eastern seaboard, and all implored him to take time from his teaching to supply written and illustrated Pyle masterpieces. The demands, coming from so many sources, of course were impossible to fulfill, and Pyle therefore offered his students' works as substitutes. At first reluctant to accept student creations in place of the master's, editors eventually agreed to his plan when Pyle assured them that he would personally supervise each creation. Selecting the best of several illustrations drawn during in-class competitions, he submitted works only if he himself was completely satisfied with their quality.

Such introductions to publishers by Pyle helped to launch several careers since entry into the portals of publishing was so often closed to a beginner. Smith's first major book illustration, Longfellow's *Evangeline*, shared with fellow student Oakley, was the direct result of an introduction by Pyle.

Pyle was wary of excessive decoration in his students' works, but he was especially partial to large expressive forms and areas which would be outlined and later filled with broad flat colors or patterns. Smith was not totally immune from this characteristic in her work, but certain artists, like Ethel Franklin Betts, Anna Whelan Betts, Charlotte Harding, and Sarah Stilwell made especially strong use of this feature in their respective works.

Smith, Green, and Oakley were very conscious of decoration. The deeply brocaded gown, the patterned wall paper, the heavily decorated chair, these became characteristics that set Pyle's female students apart from their male counterparts. Early works by Smith and Green are remarkably similar. So too are the work of Charlotte Harding and the post-Pyle work of Alice Barber Stephens. Pyle's male students often left the area for New York and other cities in which they could develop their art on their own. The women instead remained close-knit. For years after the Pyle lessons had ended, Smith, Oakley, and Green shared the same home. Harding and Stephens, who remained in the Philadelphia area, were regular guests at Cogslea, and since all were employed in the same trade, it is likely that their frequent visits contained discussions and comparisons of each woman's recent creation.

The early 1900s offered much more mobility to a young working male than to a female, and these young artists therefore formed what could be called a self-propelling school of art. Admittedly, it was Pyle's teaching that brought them together, and we could then dub them quite properly the Brandywine Women. Years after his teachings were done they continued to develop into a force and style that grew out of each other's variation from the mean, a force in American illustration that has not yet received its proper recognition.

The careers of some of the Brandywine women artists, serving as an introduction to the work of the group as a whole, are examined here briefly. Special emphasis is placed on Green, Emerson, and Oakley because of their close living and working relationships with Smith. These brief biographical sketches, with their accompanying illustrations, are flagrantly designed to show that this group of women artists is truly worthy of a major published study.

Elenore Plaisted Abbott

One of the more active children's book illustrators to graduate from Pyle's Drexel classes, Abbott was born in Lincoln, Maine, in 1875, and she eventually settled in Philadelphia. Like Smith, her artistic training began at the School of Design for Women and the Academy. She left for two years of study in Paris, and, after her return to Philadelphia, she enrolled in Pyle's class at Drexel, quickly landing illustration commissions. Her first major work was illustrating a 1911 edition of *Treasure Island*. During her career she illustrated other children's classics including *Robinson Crusoe* (1913), *Grimm's Fairy Tales* (1922), and Alcott's *An Old Fashioned Girl* (1926). She married C. Yarnell Abbott, a painter, and was a member of the Plastic Club of Philadelphia and the Philadelphia Watercolor Club.

Ellen Wetherald Ahrens

One of Smith's friends at the Academy, she briefly shared the 1523 Chestnut Street studio with her, Dodd, and Oakley. She never achieved the fame of some of the others. Born in Baltimore, Ahrens first studied at the Boston Museum of Fine Arts. She continued at the Academy with Eakins, later joining Smith and the others at Drexel. Though she at first attempted an illustration career, her interest in portrait painting and miniatures took her to Pittsburgh's Carnegie Institute for further study. She obtained several awards during her career, including the Second Toppan Prize of the Academy (1884), the Silver Medal of the Carnegie Institute (1901), and bronze medals for oil painting and miniatures at

25. Anna Whelan Betts, a typical illustration showing her characteristic ingenue in nineteenth century costume

the 1904 St. Louis Exposition. Ahrens never married and settled in Lansdowne, Pennsylvania.

Ethel Franklin Betts (Bains)
Like the Cogslea artists, Betts shared a studio with another Pyle student, Dorothy Warren. While they studied illustration with the master at Drexel, she attended courses at the Academy. An active illustrator of children's books, she illustrated James Whitcomb Riley's *The Raggedy Man* (1907) and *Mother Goose* (1909) among others. Her illustration for the story "The Six Swans" won a bronze medal at the Panama/Pacific International Exposition in 1915. An occasional contributor of cover art for *Collier's*, Betts was also a member of the Philadelphia Water Color Club. She married late in her career.

26. Elizabeth Shippen Green, illustration for *The Book of the Child,* 1903.

Anna Whelan Betts
Sister of Ethel, she was best known for her romantic illustrations of young Victorian women on the threshold of their first romance. Born in Philadelphia, she attended Pyle's class at Drexel and the Chadds Ford summer class in 1899, where her fellow students included Bertha Corson Day, Ellen Thomson, and Sara Stillwell. During her first summer at Chadds Ford, she created a series of drawings for a novel, *Janice Meredith*. Later she did illustrations for *Harper's Century, McClure's,* and *St. Nicholas.* She received the bronze medal at the Panama/Pacific Exposition and was a member of the Philadelphia Water Color Club.

Elizabeth Fearne Bonsall
Best known as a painter of animals, Bonsall first studied at the Academy under

27. Elizabeth Shippen Green, illustration for *The Book of the Child,* 1903.

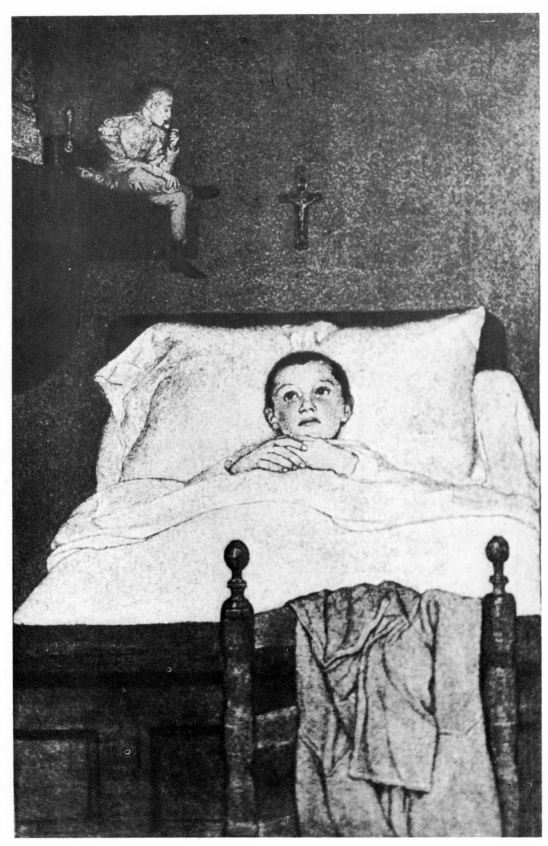

28. Elizabeth Shippen
Green, " 'I am
accustomed to
Precipices,' the wooden
soldier would answer,"
from "Aurelie,"
Harper's Monthly,
September, 1909

Eakins and then in Paris before joining Pyle's Drexel class. Twice awarded the Academy's Mary Smith Prize, in 1888 and 1897, Bonsall had previously received the First Toppan Prize of the Academy in 1885. She settled in Philadelphia and was widely known through her activities with the Plastic Club, the Academy Fellowship, the Art Alliance, and the Print Club.

Ethel Pennewill Brown (Leach)

This Wilmington-born illustrator studied with the American impressionist, John H. Twachtman and at the Ecole Moderne in Paris before returning to the Wilmington area to join Pyle's classes, which he established in that city in 1900 after his second summer of classes at Chadds Ford. Brown made a specialty of local landscapes. Her illustrations for Katherine Pyle's *Once Upon a Time in Delaware* are among her best known works. After her marriage to William Leach, she settled in Frederica, Delaware. When Pyle left for Italy in 1911, she was one of the students entrusted with the care and keeping of his studio while he was away. During the summer months, Leach promoted art activities in Rehoboth, Delaware, while during the remaining months she was active in the Wilmington Society of the Fine Arts, the Philadelphia Art Alliance, the Academy Fellowship, the Plastic Club, and the Print Club.

Charlotte Harding Brown

In 1947, the acquisitive American illustrator and collector, Thornton Oakley, wrote to his friend Charlotte Harding Brown and asked if she had any of her original illustrations which she would be willing to sell him for his collection of American illustrator art. Her unfortunate reply was that, outside of a few drawings that had personal meaning, "everything else went into a bonfire. I had no reason to keep anything, for that phase of my life had ended years before."[40]

Such a tragic loss of an important illustrator's work only reaffirms the need to reconsider the ridiculous pretention that art is art and illustration is illustration and ne'er the twain shall meet.

Pyle had little patience with people who promulgated such philosophy, and would have been horrified to know that one of his star pupils had so little regard for her own works that she found a bonfire preferable to keeping her illustrations on hand. This loss is especially great because Brown was among the best known and most prolific of Pyle's female students. She was also among those who gave effective dimension to his teaching in her work.

A protege of Alice Barber Stephens, who shared a studio with this other important illustrator, Brown worked for dozens of publications from the turn of the century onward including: *Harper's, Century, McClure's, Colliers, Ladies Home Journal,* and the *Saturday Evening Post*. She followed the same art education path as Smith, beginning at the School of Design for Women, then continuing at the Academy and finding herself with Pyle at Drexel. A close friend of the Cogslea women, she married James Adams Brown, a mechanical engineer, in 1905. But unlike some women illustrators who let marriage put a virtual halt to their careers, Brown continued to work and to win awards. She obtained medals at both the St. Louis Exposition and the Panama/Pacific Exposition.

This Newark-born illustrator was active in the Philadelphia Water Color Club, the Plastic Club, the Academy Fellowship, and other city groups. Primarily a magazine illustrator, she preferred adolescents to children as subjects, and she was most comfortable in the medium of charcoal. She died at age 78 in Smithtown, Long Island where she had settled shortly after the death of her husband.

Bertha Corson Day (Bates)

Day attended art classes at Drexel before Pyle began teaching there. She traveled to England in 1898, but on her return to America, she came back to Drexel for Pyle's classes. She developed a strong friendship with Pyle and his family and was selected to illustrate Katherine Pyle's book, *Where the Wind Blows*. A frequent designer of posters, she was a member of the Philadelphia Water Color Club, the Plastic Club, the Print Club, and the Art Alliance. In 1902 she married Daniel Moore Bates and discontinued her professional career.

Edith Emerson

Emerson was never a student of Howard Pyle and would therefore be an unlikely candidate for inclusion in a study of the Brandywine women. But the Pyle teachings appear in her works as surely as if she had personally had the benefit of his tutelage. A protege of Oakley who lived for several years in the Cogslea household, Emerson had the benefit of watching Pyle's teachings being put to practical use by Smith and Oakley.

As a pupil at the Art Institute of Chicago, Emerson heard Pyle lecture and was so impressed that she investigated the opportunities available to her in the Philadelphia area. She moved to that city in 1913 and enrolled in the Academy where she studied portrait painting with Cecilia Beaux and mural decoration with Violet Oakley. Her exceptional talents as a muralist became clear very quickly, and she was awarded a Cresson Scholarship in 1914 and 1915 for a period of study abroad.

Active in a number of Philadelphia organizations, she participated in the Philadelphia Art Alliance, the Society of Mural Painters, the Philadelphia Water Color Club, the American Federation of Arts, the American Society of Bookplate Collectors and Designers, and the Artists' League of Germantown. Her murals and stained glass creations decorate the Plays and Players Theatre in Philadelphia; Temple Keneseth Israel; the Moorestown, New Jersey Trust Company; and the Haverford, Pennsylvania Preparatory School.

After Elizabeth Shippen Green Elliott's departure from Cogslea, she joined Oakley there where she served as personal aide and continued her art studies with her. After Oakley's death in 1961, Emerson founded the Violet Oakley Memorial Foundation, dedicated to the preservation and promulgation of Oakley's works and philosophy. She currently resides in Cogslea, where she devotes herself to community activities.

Elizabeth Shippen Green (Elliott)

Among her friends, Green was best remembered for her immense good humor and her quick wit. On a page of the Friendship Calendar given to Jessie Dowd,

Green made an amusing reference to Pyle. Mocking his authoritative manner, she invented a quote from the master: "Now, Miss Dodd, don't you see, just as soon as I touch my brush to your drawing, how much better it becomes?"[41]

The affectionate joke was made in good spirit, for even when she wrote it in 1900, Green was already aware of Pyle's vital importance to her career. Of all the Brandywine women, she, more than most, brought Pyle's teachings into perfect visual form. Her sense of composition was deeply akin to Pyle's: broad expanses in some areas of a picture which cleverly directed the viewer's attention to the less centralized, but more important, featured attraction; rich, bright colors; and a special fascination with medieval subjects which developed into a scholarly appreciation of costumes and other details that repeatedly appear in her works.

This Philadelphia born artist was fortunate in that both her parents were lovers of art and that she was encouraged to pursue an art career. Educated in private schools, she entered the Academy in 1887, studying there with Robert Vonnoh and Thomas Eakins. After graduation from the Academy at age 18 she began illustrating for various Philadelphia newspapers and then the Strawbridge and Clothier department store. In 1895 she took a staff post at *The Ladies' Home Journal,* and in the following year enrolled in Pyle's Drexel classes. It was here that she met Smith and Oakley and in 1897 was invited to join them in their 1523 Chestnut Street studio. Green was still living with her parents at the time, but the convivial atmosphere and budding professional relationships at the women's studios made great sense to her. After a European journey, she joined the other women.

Green combined her own initiative with Pyle's help in finding assignments to become one of the most prolific illustrators of the period. Her works appeared regularly in *The Saturday Evening Post, The Ladies' Home Journal,* and the young person's magazines, *Forward* and *The Scholar's Magazine.* In 1901, Green began a semi-exclusive contract with *Harper's* that would continue until 1924. This diminished her activities for other magazines and she was able to devote more time to book illustration, volumes generally directed toward children or young teens.

She summered with Oakley and Smith at Bryn Mawr in 1901 and finally made a home for herself and her parents at the Red Rose Inn. At that time her close friend Henrietta Cozens also joined the group, and they all moved together to Cogslea in 1905. This was also the year in which she met Huger Elliott, the Philadelphia architect who called her "the Greatest Illustrator of the Age" and who wasted no time in proposing marriage. They became man and wife in 1912 after the deaths of Green's parents. She travelled extensively with her husband, settling in various locations as he advanced to each new prominent position. First the Director of the Rhode Island School of Design and then the Director of the Philadelphia College of Art, he was later named Director of the education department of the Metropolitan Museum in New York. The Elliotts remained there until his death in 1951 when she returned to Philadelphia, remaining until her death three years later.

While so many relocations on behalf of her husband would have dampened the spirits of most career women, Green only made it part of her own success,

29. Charlotte Harding, "Theodora was elegantly sauntering down the stairs," from *Harper's Monthly*

30. Elizabeth Shippen Green, "A Picnic," advertising illustration for the Dana Manufacturing Company, c. 1910

developing contacts with publishers all over the east. Her new relationships with publishers led to more book illustration. Among her most successful books were her illustrated version of Charles and Mary Lamb's *Tales from Shakespeare* (1922) and the immensely pleasing *An Alliterative Alphabet Aimed at Adult Abecedarians* (1947), on which she collaborated with her husband.

Margaretta S. Hinchman
A well-respected landscape artist and illustrator, Hinchman also achieved some standing as a muralist. In addition to studies with Pyle, she studied with the illustrator Kenyon Cox. Hinchman was awarded the Philadelphia Plastic Club's Silver Medal in 1927, and in 1935 she received the Academy's Mary Smith Prize. This Philadelphian was active in the American Federation of Arts, the Arts and Crafts Guild of Philadelphia, the Philadelphia Art Alliance, Water Color Club and Mural Painters.

Violet Oakley
A relative of Henrietta Cozens, who had many occasions to visit Cogslea, once stated that living with Violet Oakley was "like living in a thundercloud."[42] This idea was not far from accurate. A strong woman with deep religious con-

victions, Oakley was the cornerstone of Cogslea in many ways, serving as the matriarchal head of the household.

Oakley once stated that she was "born with a paint brush instead of a silver spoon" in her mouth.[43] Over a dozen members of her family were professional artists and the artistic roots held fast in the soil of family tradition. Arthur Edmund Oakley and William Swain, her grandfathers, were Associates of the National Academy of Design, and when she began her formal art studies at the Art Students' League in New York City, she received full encouragement from her family. She had early opportunity for European study because she had relatives in England where she visited during her youth. Her family was therefore primed for her eventual departure for Paris after one year at the League. In Paris she attended the Academie Montparnasse where she studied art with the French symbolist painter, Edmond Aman-Jean, and with Raphael Colin. In England she studied with Charles Lasar, an artist whose emphasis on decorative design had a lasting effect on her work. It was probably during this time that Oakley became acquainted with the work of Sir Edward Burne-Jones and other pre-Raphaelite English painters whose mystical canvases later were echoed in her own works.

Returning to Philadelphia in 1896, Oakley enrolled in the Academy, while her sister, Hester, attended Pyle's Drexel class. Her family had moved to Philadelphia from South Orange, New Jersey, but art education was not the sole reason for the move. Arthur Edmund Oakley, Violet's father, was suffering from a severe illness and the move to Philadelphia was thought necessary because of the proximity to medical specialists in that city. Her father's lingering illness proved very painful to the impressionable young woman, and she was quickly disillusioned with the medical science which did so little for him. She had also been plagued with asthma since childhood and few medicines brought relief. It was at this time that Mary Baker Eddy's Christian Science Church was gaining converts and Oakley, though her family was Episcopalian, turned to the new religion. In it she found the peace to help ease her asthma.

While at the Academy, Oakley studied with Cecilia Beaux, Joseph DeCamp and Henry Thouron. Her sister, however, urged her to join Pyle's class at Drexel, and in 1897 she did just that, meeting Smith and Green. Oakley, the youngest of the three women, was by contrast the most serious. Her father had recently died and she was left with an aging mother who had a small income and life had hit her rather severely.

Pyle, immediately recognizing her talent, teamed her with Smith for *Evangeline*, but aware of her strong religious faith and the natural decorative qualities of her work, suggested that she try stained glass. She followed his advice and in a short time had created the design for a stained glass window for the Church Glass and Decorating Company in New York. Her next major project was a two-year effort – two murals, a mosaic reredos and five stained glass windows for the Church of All Angels in New York City. During this time she also designed a stained glass window for the Convent of the Holy Child at Sharon Hill, Pennsylvania.

A wealth of new building projects at the turn of the century gave Oakley

31. *The Book of the Child,* 1902

JESSIE WILLCOX SMITH,

32. *The Book of the Child,*
1902

33. *The Book of the Child,*
1902

34. "Picture Books in Winter," *A Child's Garden of Verses*, 1905

35. "The Hayloft," *A Child's Garden of Verses*, 1905

36. "I can build a castle to the sky," *Dream Blocks*, 1908

FOREIGN CHILDREN

37. "Foreign Children," *A Child's Garden of Verses*, 1905

(71)

JESSIE WILLCOX SMITH.

Copyright, 1908, by Duffield & Co.

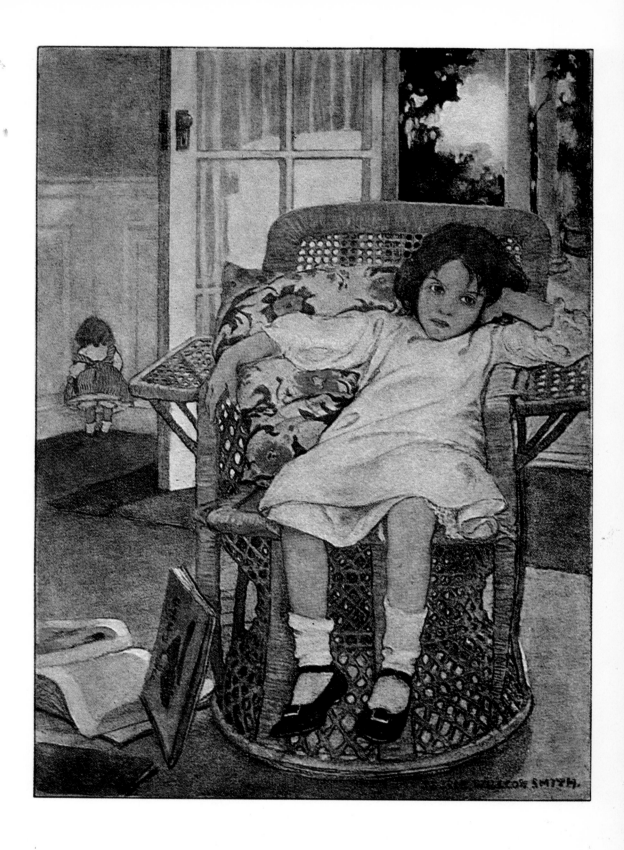

40. "Rainy Day,"
Dream Blocks, 1908

41. "A Modern
Cinderella," *The Now-
A-Days Fairy Book,* 1911 ▶

(75)

42. "Robin Put His
Head Down on His
Arm, and Shut His
Eyes," *The Now-A-
Days Fairy Book,* 1911

SHE LUFS ME — SHE LUFS ME NOT —

43. "She Lufs Me – She
Lufs Me Not," *The
Now-A-Days Fairy Book,*
1911

44. "Tom reached and clawed down the hole after him," *The Water Babies,* 1916

45. "He felt the net very ▶ heavy and lifted it out quickly, with Tom all entangled in the meshes," *The Water Babies,* 1916

JESSIE WILLCOX SMITH.

ample opportunity to practice her skills. One major project was the new Pennsylvania Capitol building in Harrisburg, designed by the architect Joseph M. Houston. One newspaper of the time reported, "Mr. Houston's recommendation that one of the rooms be decorated by a woman artist. He names Miss Violet Oakley 'purely because of the superior excellence of her work'."[44] While the gesture was certainly magnanimous, the article went on to add that Houston proposed "that one of the rooms of minor importance be entrusted to Miss Oakley. . . ."[45]

The room in question was the Governor's reception room, hardly a minor project, since 18 murals were involved and the work took four years to complete. After a short study trip abroad, Oakley returned to Pennsylvania to begin the murals, which were based on the life of the state's founder, William Penn. In 1905 her murals won her the Academy's Gold Medal, the first woman to be so honored since 1898 when Cecilia Beaux was the first woman to be awarded the coveted prize.

In 1911 Oakley was asked to complete the late Edwin Abbey's murals for the Senate Chambers and Supreme Court at the capitol. She worked until 1920 to complete the nine major murals, but she also found time for other projects. These included a painting, "The Constitutional Convention," for the new Cuyahoga County Court House in Cleveland, Ohio; a mural called "Great Women of the Bible" for the First Presbyterian Church of Germantown, Pennsylvania; and a mural for the Philadelphia High School for Girls.

During the last decades of the 1800s and the first of the 1900s, she also drew cover and story illustrations for *Century, Collier's, The Ladies' Home Journal,* and other publications. Most of her illustrations were of a religious or spiritual nature and often appeared in conjunction with such holidays as Easter or Christmas. Despite her active illustration schedule, she did not consider herself a true illustrator and resigned from New York's Society of Illustrators in 1922.

Oakley was a strong believer in world disarmament, a concept which encouraged her firm support of the League of Nations. From 1927 to 1929 she attended that body's Geneva meetings and painted portraits of many of the delegates. Other portrait commissions were infrequent, but they included such notables as Queen Sophia of Greece; Catherine Drinker Bowen, the author; and Albert Spalding, the concert violinist.

Oakley was also a highly professional promoter of her own work and causes. She self-published bound volumes of reproductions of her murals, including *The Holy Experiment,* which featured her state capitol designs. The 300-copy limited edition book featured handsome calligraphy and decorations by the artist. Her immense talent for calligraphy and illumination encouraged Smith to nickname her "Elaborate Violet."[46]

Her rich and vibrant career did not go unappreciated by her contemporaries. In addition to the Academy's Gold Medal of Honor, Oakley was awarded an Honorary Doctor of Laws Degree by Drexel Institute in 1948. Until her death in 1961, Oakley was actively engaged in numerous projects, and the greater part of her life was spent at Cogslea.

46. "And Tom sat upon the buoy long days," *The Water Babies,* 1916

Ellen Bernard Thompson (Pyle)

When Ellen Thompson was a young art student at Pyle's Chadds Ford summer class, she met and eventually married his younger brother, Walter. He died in 1919, leaving her with a young family to support and her art career which she had only pursued in moderation before marriage. Thereafter, her rosy-cheeked youngsters made frequent appearances on the covers of *The Saturday Evening Post* and other publications.

Katherine Pyle

The sister of Howard Pyle, she collaborated with her brother on *The Wonder Clock*, which he wrote and illustrated and which she embellished with verses. This 1888 volume was the first of several works she wrote and illustrated, a formidable list which includes such titles as *Heroic Tales from Greek Mythology*, *Wonder Tales Retold*, and *Charlemagne and his Knights*. A writer of children's verses, she also collaborated with Bertha Corson Day on her book, *Where the Wind Blows*.

Born in Wilmington, Pyle studied at the Women's Industrial School in that city and later joined her brother's class at Drexel, finally continuing her studies at the Art Students' League in New York. An expert historian whose illustrations reflect sound research, she decreased her activity as an illustrator and devoted herself to portraiture late in her career.

Olive Rush

This Indiana-born artist was a student of John Twachtman at New York's Art Students' League before she left for Paris, where she studied and exhibited her works at the annual Salon. She later attended Pyle's Wilmington classes and concentrated on mural decoration. One of her earliest commissions was the altar decoration for St. Andrew's Church in Wilmington. Later she painted murals for the La Fonda Hotel and the Public Library of Santa Fe, New Mexico. When Pyle left Wilmington for Italy in 1911, she was one of the students entrusted with the care of his studios. Late in her career Rush made a speciality of children's and women's portraits. A member of the New York Watercolor Club and the Wilmington Society of the Fine Arts, she was recipient of several awards.

Waunita Smith

An illustrator and graphic artist, Smith's illustrated books include *Gulliver's Travels, Grimms Fairy Tales,* and others. Before study with Pyle at Drexel, she studied at the School of Design for Women, the Academy, and the Art Students' League under Hugh Breckenridge. Later she studied in Paris. Smith settled in Philadelphia and was active in a number of art clubs.

Alice Barber Stephens

Anyone who doubts the profound effect of Pyle's teaching need only compare the illustrative work of Stephens before she joined his Drexel classes with those created after. Early in her career, Stephens was a wood engraver for *Scribner's*

47. Violet Oakley, cover, *Everybody's Magazine,* June, 1902

(83)

one of the first women to achieve such a post with a major magazine. Her talent
for illustration quickly advanced her from the rigorous copying routine of the
wood engraver to a formidable career as an illustrator for *Century, Harper's*
and *Scribner's.* Her drawings, usually done in pen and ink, were of humble
genre subjects which reiterated the fine line techniques she had employed as an
engraver.

The change in her work after study with Pyle is so dramatic that one would
hardly assume her illustrations were by the same artist. Stephen's forms became
bolder and larger. She abandoned excessive detail in favor of broad areas of

(86)

50. Sara S. Stillwell,
"A New Day," from
*Luxuries of Children and
Some Other Luxuries,*
1905

color and heavy outline. Her composition was more daring than it had ever been. Stephens initially joined Pyle's classes to satisfy her curiosity about the remarkable man. She was over a decade older than most of the students, but her professional understanding of the problems and methods he discussed aided her in applying his concepts to her illustrative work. She was born in Salem, New Jersey, and her family moved to Philadelphia during her youth. Her art studies began at the School of Design for Women and she later studied at the Academy. In Paris, she studied at the Academie Julian, and she found work for *Scribner's* when she returned. She later joined the faculty of the School of Design for Women as a teacher of portrait painting and life drawing. Before assuming this post, she met and married the Philadelphia artist, Charles Stephens, who encouraged her career. She continued her magazine illustrating after studying with Pyle, but like many of his students, she also began to illustrate books. The titles she highlighted with her art range from Alcott's *Little Women* to Wiggin's *Mother Carey's Chickens*. Her magazine credits were weighty and a series of illustrations of famous American women in *The Ladies' Home Journal* brought her great public attention. She was honored with the Academy's Mary Smith Prize in 1890 and later won a Bronze Medal at the Atlanta Exposition.

Sara S. Stillwell (Weber)

A Sara Stillwell drawing is an excursion into the most delightful fantasy. Her covers for *Collier's* often feature children dancing in fairy gardens or exotic ladies floating in seas of splendid imagery. Stillwell first studied with Pyle at Drexel and then joined him for the 1899 summer session at Chadd's Ford, later studying with him in Wilmington. She illustrated a number of books for children, including *The Luxury of Children* and *Some Other Luxuries* by Edward Sandford Martin. In almost all her work, oil was the exclusive medium. She and her husband settled in Philadelphia, although they traveled frequently to Nova Scotia for summer vacations.

The above biographies are but a brief introduction to only a few women students of Howard Pyle. Their status as illustrators of children's books or for periodicals at the turn of the century had determined their inclusion here. Like Smith, these women applied their talent to the teachings of Howard Pyle, leaving a published legacy of works that is a sound tribute to the amazing mark that he left on American illustration.

3·A Child's Garden
Illustrated Books

J ESSIE Willcox Smith is known primarily as an illustrator of books for children, but in truth her books appealed as much to adult tastes as to those of younger readers. In one of her books, given as a gift to a child who posed for one of her paintings, she wrote, "To Pierre – With the understanding that if he finds this book too young for his advanced years – he shall give to his father. With love, Jessie Willcox Smith."[47]

Smith did not consciously attempt to appeal to adults but her insight into children permeated her pictures, and it was best understood by those who had children of their own and could relate the playtime activities of their youngsters to Smith's models. But children were not her first subjects, and several books of illustrations preceded her first "children's book."

Her first book illustrations appeared with Oakley's in *Evangeline*. Their paintings were converted to chromolithographs, a popular color reproduction process of the period, and though the illustrations show the unmistakable stamp of Pyle's teaching, they do not predict the future direction of either woman's illustration. *Evangeline* was an adult love story, ending in tragedy, a work whose historical flavor would perhaps have better suited Elizabeth Shippen Green. Coming on the heels of dozens of similar illustrated volumes of narrative poetry the book was not a commercial success, but it did represent Smith's introduction to book illustration. With Howard Pyle's help, Smith and Oakley proved that they could hold their own against most of the book illustrators of the time.

Evangeline was followed by Smith's infamous Indian illustrations to which she referred often without actually naming the works. She probably meant *The Head of the Hundred* by Maud Wilder Goodwin, a love story of Colonial America. Though she objected to painting Indians, her illustrations for this work show insight and power, and it is easy to understand why the publisher again requested more such illustrations from this young woman artist.

Her next books were written by Nathaniel Hawthorne, *Tales and Sketches* and *Mosses from an Old Manse*. Again these works were adult subject matter, a field of illustration in which Smith was perfectly competent, but in which she did not feel completely at ease. It was not until her "Brenda" books that Smith began to reach for a more suitable forum for her illustrations. Sentimental romances directed at the pre-teen reader, *Brenda, Her School and Her Club,* and *Brenda's*

51. " 'Now then fall to, ladies, and help yourself'," An Old Fashioned Girl, 1902

(88)

Summer at Rockley, could hardly be considered literature, but the books gave Smith the opportunity to illustrate contemporary subjects and to use young women acquaintances as models. Her illustrations for these works were pleasant, but forgettable; but they gave her a taste of subject matter that would at last involve her deeply in book illustration.

Little, Brown & Company, who had developed her "Brenda" books, approached Smith in 1901 about doing illustrations for Louisa May Alcott's *An Old Fashioned Girl*. Originally published in 1870, this work had already gone through several editions, and it was one of the most popular girls' books of its time, a classic of its genre. Smith was delighted with the opportunity, and set to work on twelve charcoal illustrations for the book. Though young women feature prominently in the illustrations, this was also Smith's first opportunity to include children in book illustrations, and these are the most appealing of all

53. "So Polly tucked herself up in front," An Old Fashioned Girl, 1902

54. "Seven times one,"
A Child's Book of Old Verses, 1910

the illustrations. The dramatic perspective of youngsters tobogganing is striking in its generous use of white space, while a children's visit to the elderly matriarch of the family has a pleasant appeal of its own. In another picture, that of an afternoon tea, one can well imagine similar occasions that were a daily affair at the Red Rose Inn or Cogslea.

This work was published in 1902, but one of Smith's foremost accomplishments would occur during the following year. *The Child,* a calendar collaboration with Elizabeth Shippen Green, a privately invested project, became so popular that it was immediately reprinted by the Frederick A. Stokes Company as *The Book of the Child,* after an addition of text by Mabel Humphrey. By far Smith's most appealing pictures to date, these illustrations opened the way for her first children's book, a volume intended primarily for the enjoyment of children and not adult buyers. This was *Rhymes of Real Children* by Elizabeth Sage Goodwin, the first of many such poetry compendiums that would bear Smith's name as illustrator.

55. "This Little Land,"
A Child's Garden of Verses, 1905

(92)

In 1904, McClure Phillips Company published *In the Closed Room* by Frances Hodgson Burnett, a story that originally appeared in *McClure's* Magazine. This was the first time that Smith's illustrations served a dual purpose, first published in a periodical and then being called into action again for a book. In sensitive illustrations, which were obviously posed in the richly interesting interiors of the Red Rose Inn, Smith chronicled the concern of a little girl for her sickly friend.

By 1905, the date of publication of *A Child's Garden of Verses* by Robert Louis Stevenson, Smith had achieved a positive imprint in the mind of the reading public. *Scribner's,* who published this new work, and spared no expense for printing, commissioned Smith to provide numerous line illustrations as well as ten color paintings. Her works recalled moments of childhood common to everyone, whether lived in reality or imagined in fantasy. It was simple to relate to "Picture Books in Winter," or "My Shadow." No doubt countless children's imaginings were sparked by the bed ridden boy in "The Land of Counterpane" or the brave explorer in "Northwest Passage."

Thus began an important aspect of Smith's book illustration which might be called her series illustrations. Most of the illustrated books produced during her career fall into this category, volumes that include poems or stories with accompanying illustrations. The appendix lists these various works, some of which were developed by the publishers and others by Smith herself. Among the most notable of these series works is *Dream Blocks* by Aileen C. Higgins, which in 1908 featured the same dust jacket illustration, "Mother and Child," which appears on this volume. Later series illustrations included *Boys and Girls of Bookland* by Nora Archibald Smith and *The Children of Dickens* compiled by Samuel McChord Crothers.

Smith's fertile imagination enabled her to continually supply a generous scope of settings and situations for her pictures which combined her artistry with another vital element: her inescapable warmth. One critic commented at the time of her greatest popularity:

> Miss Smith has created for us more of a type of childhood. There is no mistaking a drawing or painting by this artist: that charm in children that appeals to all pervades her work, and, although it is essentially illustrative in its rendering, a high order of craftsmanship is displayed. There is no better nor significant way to describe the irresistible charm of Miss Smith's work than to say its spirit is akin to that which pervades Stevenson's *A Child's Garden of Verse*. . . . On the seashore, or in the fields, Miss Smith asks us to join her little army at play; but if we do, we must leave behind anything not distinctly of the child's world, for these little people will be intolerant of the artificial.[48]

Said another, "It is a long road from the smudgy heavy lines outlining expressionless little girls in pinafores and pantalets, and lads in long trousers and flat caps, to the round, deliciously human figures of children in such books as we regard, 'adapted to the ideas of children' in our day; a long road with a pleasant ending."[49]

In some cases, Smith generated her own ideas for series books, compiling

56. "Beauty and the Beast," *The Now-A-Days Fairy Book*, 1911.

them and gathering editorial materials together herself. *The Child's Stamp Book of Old Verses,* published by Duffield in 1915, was such a work. In *Mother Goose,* Smith joined together the pictures she had done for *Good Housekeeping* between 1912 and 1918, making an irresistible package for child or adult.

Many of Smith's book illustrations had first appeared in periodicals. *Billy Boy,* published in 1906, had first been seen in *Collier's* during the previous year. The illustrations which comprised *The Seven Ages of Childhood* in 1909 had first been featured in *The Ladies' Home Journal* over a period of months during 1908 and

1909. The 1911 printing of *The Five Senses* had graduated to book form after a 1907 appearance in *McClure's Magazine*.

Smith was a clever businesswoman as well as a fine illustrator, another lesson that she no doubt learned from Howard Pyle who also instructed students on some financial aspects of illustrating for books and magazines. Usually receiving a fee for an illustration, she would attempt to obtain royalties for future use of that illustration. In some cases, she asked that the illustration be returned to her and she then sold it to the parents of the child who had posed for it. This fine business sense is a credit to her understanding of facts of the illustrating life, an understanding that played no small role in her financial stability.

In addition to her series illustrations, Smith also illustrated children's books in the narrative form where one story was illustrated by a series of pictures. Without a doubt, her illustrations for *Water Babies* by Charles Kingsley, published in 1916 and representative of this narrative illustration, are a high point in her career. A more perfect marriage of pictures and prose could hardly

58. "It took the form of ▶ the grandest old lady he had ever seen," *The Water Babies*, 1916

57. 'Twas the Night Before Christmas, 1912

59. "Mrs. Bedonebyas-
youdid," *The Water
Babies,* 1916

60. "Mrs. Doasyou-
wouldbedoneby," The
Water Babies, 1916

61. "I like little pussy,"
*A Child's Book of Old
Verses*, 1910

62. "Down the mountain
they shot like two birds
darting through the air,"
Heidi, 1922.

(101)

63. "Little Miss Muffet,"
The Little Mother Goose,
1917

64. "Peter, Peter,
Pumpkin Eater," *Good
Housekeeping,* 1917

65. "In an instant she
was on his saddle and
clasped in his great
strong arms," *The
Princess and the Goblin*,
1920

66. "Are you ill, dear
North Wind?" *At the
Back of the North Wind,*
1919

67. "She clapped her
hands with delight, and
up rose such a flapping
of wings," *The Princess
and the Goblin,* 1920

(106)

68. Cover, *Good House-
keeping,* August, 1926

Good Housekeeping

JULY 1929

25 CENTS
35 CENTS IN CANADA

JESSIE WILLCOX SMITH

A JOB FOR EVERY WOMAN
By Elizabeth Frazer — *Warwick Deeping* — *Elizabeth Petersen*
Edison Marshall — *Emma-Lindsay Squier* — *Archibald Rutledge*

69. Cover, *Good House-*
keeping, July, 1929

(108)

Good Housekeeping

MAY 1928   25 CENTS
                        15 CENTS IN CANADA

JESSIE WILLCOX SMITH

Beginning EDISON MARSHALL'S New Serial
Fanny Heaslip Lea ~ Bruce Barton ~ Philip Guedalla
Mabel W. Willebrandt ~ Jay Gelzer ~ Mrs. Francis King
INTERIOR DECORATING PAGES IN FULL COLOR

70. Cover, *Good House-
keeping,* May, 1928

Good Housekeeping

FEBRUARY
1929

25 CENTS
35 CENTS IN CANADA

Beginning Faith Baldwin's *New Novel*
Ida Tarbell ~ Ruth Suckow ~ Norma Patterson
Vera Connolly ~ Osa Johnson ~ Bruce Barton

71. Cover, *Good House-
keeping,* February, 1929

72. Cover, *Good House-keeping*, January, 1931

Good Housekeeping

MARCH 1929

25 CENTS

35 CENTS IN CANADA

SMART NEW HATS

Faith Baldwin — Owen Johnson
Margaret Sangster — Mary Lawton — Mary Synon
Frances Parkinson Keyes

73. Cover, *Good House-keeping,* March, 1929

74. "Holding on to the banisters, she put him gently away," *Little Women,* 1915

75. "And there he saw the last of the Gairfowl standing up on the Allalone stone, all alone," *The Water Babies*, 1916

be imagined. Smith herself realized the importance of the works and in order to preserve their integrity as a collection, she willed the entire series to the Library of Congress. As a result, it is the only complete set of her illustrations remaining intact. The paintings have been exhibited periodically, and in their wealth of fantasy viewers can find the most satisfying expressions of childhood dreams. The story concerns Tom, a small chimney sweep, who falls into a river and meets its many occupants in his attempt to return to land. In addition to the ten paintings that illustrate the work, Smith also created charming line drawings that show little naked babies floating in a world of seaweed and sturgeon.

76. "No, she cannot be dirty . . . she never could have been dirty," *The Water Babies*, 1916

77. "He felt how comfortable it was to have nothing on him but himself," *The Water Babies,* 1916

In another work, *'Twas the Night Before Christmas* by Clement Clark Moore, published in 1912, Smith showed a stylistic departure. In most of her color illustrations Smith used oil paint sometimes highlighted with pastels or charcoal. She was a master of mixed media techniques and she employed all the color sources that were available to her to obtain effects in her pictures. In this instance, she used only watercolor, dispensing with shading and realistic model-

78. "She ran for some distance, turned several times, and then began to be afraid," *The Princess and the Goblin,* 1920

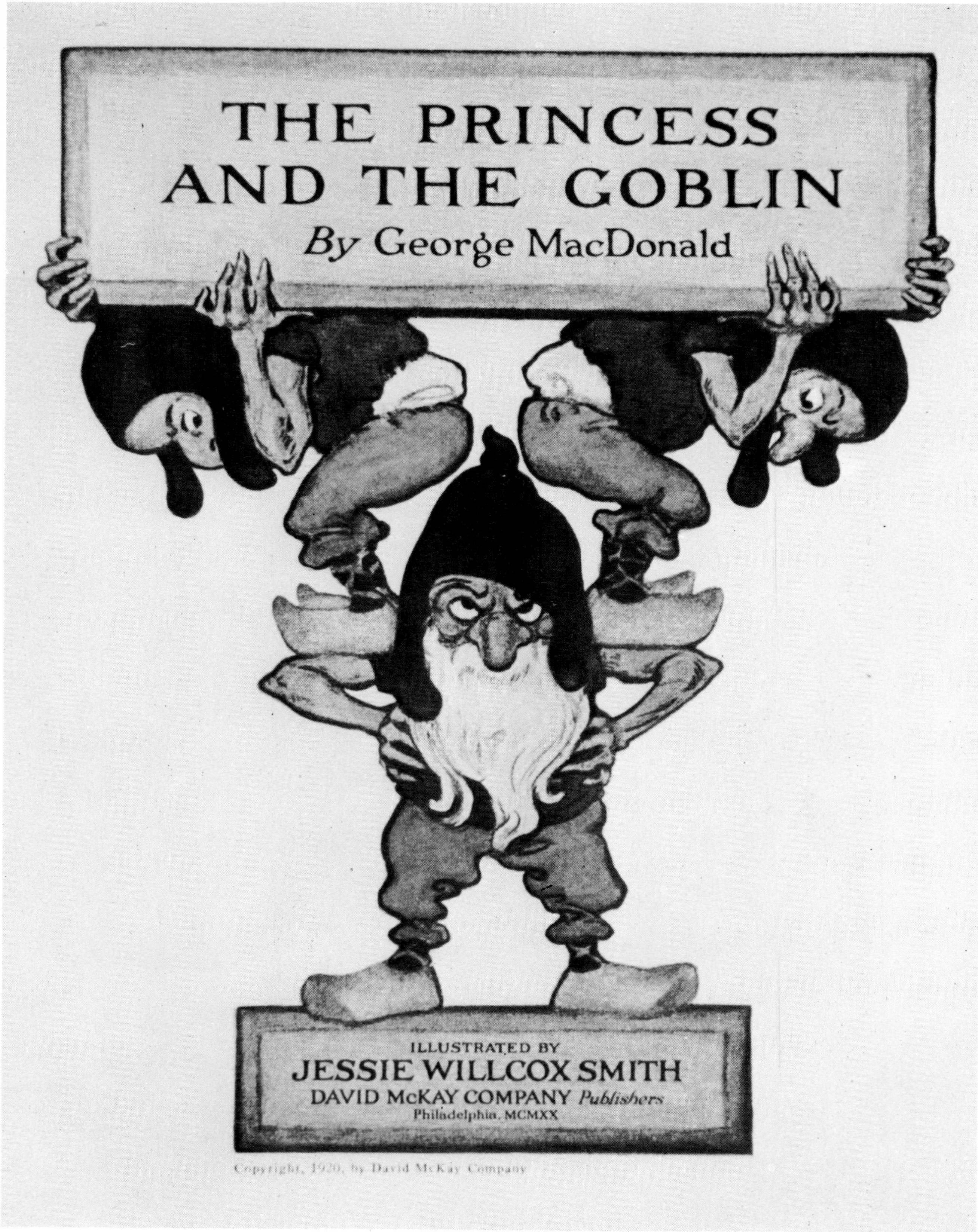
THE PRINCESS
AND THE GOBLIN
By George MacDonald
ILLUSTRATED BY
JESSIE WILLCOX SMITH
DAVID McKAY COMPANY Publishers
Philadelphia, MCMXX
Copyright, 1920, by David McKay Company

79. Title page, *The Princess and the Goblin*, 1920

80. "David Copperfield and his mother," *Boys and Girls of Bookland*, 1923

ing of her characters, relying instead on flat, bright colors to convey the poet's humorous tale of a visit from Santa Claus.

In Louisa May Alcott's *Little Women,* where Smith returned to more adult concerns in 1915, she once again proved her status as one of Howard Pyle's most successful students. Her young women seem so easily touched by the complex circumstances of their lives, as innocent in their own way as the children who populated her othe books. *Little Women* was one of Smith's most popular narrative books, but much of the credit must go to the subject itself. A popular book since its first publication in 1868, it is still being read today as one of the great children's classics.

At the Back of the North Wind and *The Princess and the Goblin,* both by George MacDonald, were published respectively in 1919 and 1920, also achieved considerable sales for the publisher, David McKay of Philadelphia. Both tales

(119)

were rich in fantasy, trips into the heavens, knights in shining armor, and other dreams of little girls and boys were fashioned by Smith into illustrations which met an eager public.

When Johanna Spyri's *Heidi* was published in 1922 with accompanying illustrations by Smith, she gave a rare interview in which she detailed the difficulty she had in finding a suitable model for the work. Heidi was described by Spyri as a dark, curly headed child, a rare commodity in Chestnut Hill where blond, straight hair decorated most of the children's heads. In order to find a model, Smith went to the public school in an Italian district of the city and explained her needs to the principal. The two then went from class to class until an appropriate Heidi was found. Smith contacted the child's mother and made

81. "Playing mother," *A Very Little Child's Book of Stories,* 1923

82. "Heidi," *Boys and Girls of Bookland,* 1923

arrangements to use her little girl as a model, but the woman was suspicious and later refused to allow her child to become Smith's Heidi. Deadlines approaching, Smith gave up her search for a substitute and relied on a neighbor's child for the paintings. As always, the illustrations were submitted on time, accepted by the publisher, and the work was a financial success. One may, however, question the artistic success of *Heidi,* since the illustrations tell their story but without the sensitivity to children that Smith had exhibited so many times in other works. Indeed, the most delightful illustration in the book does not develop character but instead shows youngsters quickly sledding down a forest hillside. The speed and twilight coloring of the picture recalls similar events in many childhoods.

Not all of Smith's illustrated books received large national distribution. For a friend she illustrated *A Child's Prayer,* a privately published work by Cora Cassard Toogood, which was distributed by David McKay Company in Philadelphia. The book of religious songs featured a cover illustration by Smith

which repeated the mother and child theme seen in one of her posters for the Philadelphia Welfare Federation. Inside she employed watercolor to capture children at prayer, a sleeping child, and other images of young innocence.

Smith stopped illustrating books in 1925. *A Child's Book of Country Stories* by the Skinner sisters was her final book. She wished to devote more time to portraiture, and enough reprint editions of her books were in circulation to provide enough income for the rest of her days.

Without question Smith revolutionized children's book illustration during the early twentieth century. Unlike Kate Greenaway, W. & F. Brundage, Randolph Caldecott, Maud Humphrey, and others who drew pleasant children with round faces and pretty bonnets, Smith created youngsters who were inescapably human. Her children were individuals with distinct personalities, recalling events that had meaning to everyone's memories of his or her own childhood.

83. "Ready for the out of doors," *A Child's Book of Country Stories,* 1925

4 · Children of the Month
Magazine Covers

ROM 1918 to 1932, the children painted by Jessie Willcox Smith appeared monthly on the covers of *Good Housekeeping Magazine*, a phenomenon that delighted millions of buyers but which was not without intrinsic hazards. Smith's children were so universal, so representative of the American youngster that the publication received numerous letters from concerned mothers in all parts of the country saying basically the same thing: "Where did you steal my child?" Mothers were absolutely convinced that the cover artist had secretly snapped their child's photograph and had used it as the basis for this nationally distributed illustration.

In some ways these bewildered parents were nearer to the truth than they suspected. For Smith's children, if one will pardon a tired expression, were the boy and girl next door. Wide-eyed, curious, as precocious as the spring crocus, they were so representative of America's ideal child that it was a rare mother who did not wish her little darling to evoke these same qualities.

One must bear in mind though that these next door types were not the ordinary run of the mill variety street urchins. In the Cogshill area, Smith's models were more likely than not from some of the wealthier families in Philadelphia, and their backgrounds were invariably evident to the keen observer. The neatly cropped and combed hair, perhaps dotted with a tasteful ribbon; the simple frock or uniform; the enviable accessories – the latest thing in teddy bears or the newest fire truck – these were the trademarks of Smith's well-heeled young models. The expensive and refined tastes of their parents helped to mold the image that indirectly would have a major effect on children everywhere in the country.

Edith Emerson once speculated that "No doubt it is largely owing to the widespread popularity of her type of children as reproduced on the covers of *Good Housekeeping* and other magazines that children's fashions have gained perceptibly in charm. Gone are the immense hair ribbons and ruffles of yester-year".[50]

One cannot be certain, of course, that her covers helped to revolutionize the children's clothing industry, but it is likely that at least a good percentage of *Good Housekeeping* readers were inclined to transform their little ones into the

84. Cover, "The First Punishment," *The Ladies' Home Journal*, January, 1905

THE LADIES' HOME JOURNAL

Vol. XXII, No. 2   PHILADELPHIA, JANUARY 1905   Yearly Subscription, One Dollar
                                                              Single Copy, Fifteen Cents

The First Punishment

By Jessie Willcox Smith

COLLIER'S

THE NATIONAL WEEKLY

HOUSEHOLD NUMBER FOR MARCH

VOL XXXIV NO 22   FEBRUARY 25 1905   PRICE 10 CENTS

86. Cover, "The First ▶
Sermon," *The Ladies'
Home Journal,* April, 1905

85. Cover, *Collier's,*
February 25, 1905

well-behaved examples fashioned by Smith, and the most logical place to begin
was appearance. Who knows how many children suddenly found themselves in
more demure outfits after their mothers began their subscriptions to *Good
Housekeeping?*

    The exceptionally-garbed children she immortalized were not the sole reason
for the success of her cover illustrations. Her own insight and clever manipula-
tion of the youngsters who posed helped to make the pictures more effective

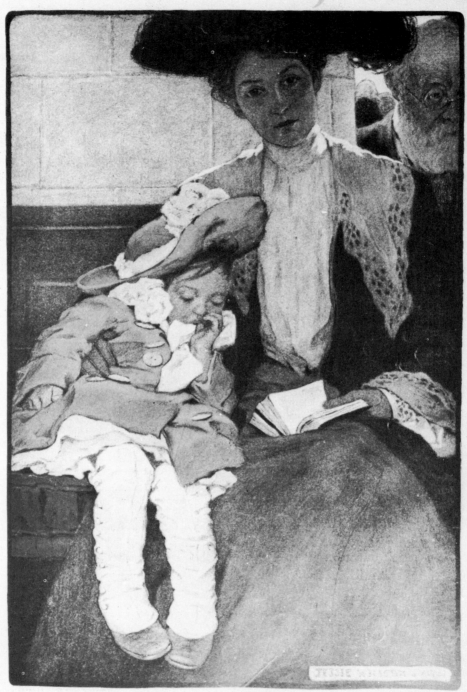

WITH 12 STORIES, MUSIC AND FASHIONS

THE LADIES' HOME JOURNAL

APRIL, 1905   THE FIRST SERMON   15 CENTS

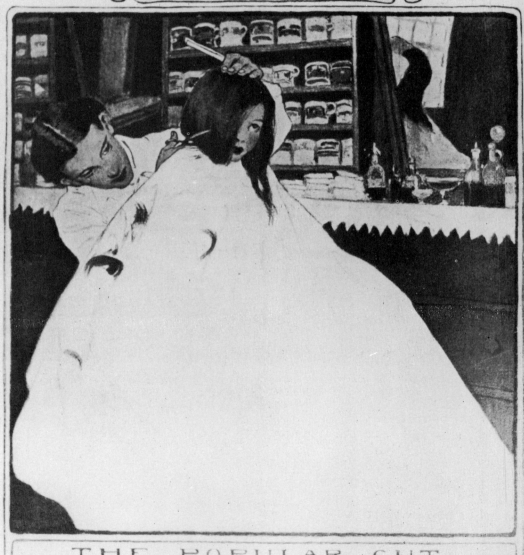

Colliers
THE NATIONAL WEEKLY

TRAGEDIES
OF CHILDHOOD

THE HURT FINGER

87. Cover, "Tragedies
of Childhood – The
Popular Cut," *Colliers,*
February 24, 1906

88. Cover, "Tragedies
of Childhood – The
Hurt Finger," *Collier's,*
April 28, 1906

Colliers

THE NATIONAL WEEKLY

JESSIE WILLCOX SMITH

HOUSEHOLD NUMBER FOR FEBRUARY

VOL XXXVI NO 18   JANUARY 27 1906   PRICE 10 CENTS

89. Cover, *Collier's,*
January 27, 1906

90. Cover, *Collier's,* ▶
June 30, 1906

COMEDIES
OF CHILDHOOD

JACK IN THE BOX !

91. Cover, "Comedies of Childhood – Jack in the Box," *Collier's*, November 24, 1906

and natural looking. Smith was, after all, fortunate in her choice of homes. The Red Rose Inn, Cogslea, and Cogshill were abundant with interesting nooks and corners where children loved to play, and thanks to Henrietta Cozens, who could almost make a pine tree blossom, the richly flowered gardens at each residence were a wonderful inspiration for youngsters to behave naturally.

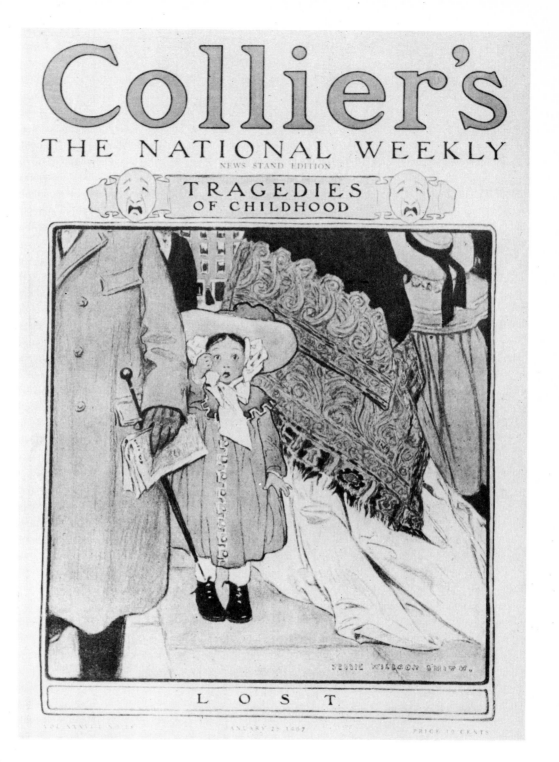

92. Cover, "Tragedies of Childhood – Lost," *Collier's,* January 26, 1907

" . . . and while they were playing at having a perfect time," Smith wrote, "I would watch and study them, and try to get them to take unconsciously the positions that I happened to be wanting for a picture. All the models I have ever had for my illustrations are just the adorable children of my kind friends, who would lend them to me for a little while."[51]

Collier's
THE NATIONAL WEEKLY

THE MARCH WIND

Asked if she ever turned to professional child models for her pictures, Smith was adamant in her distaste for them. "Such a thing as a paid and trained child model is an abomination and a travesty on childhood – a poor little crushed and scared, unnatural atom, automatically taking the pose and keeping it in a spiritless, lifeless manner. The professional child model is usually a horribly self-conscious, overdressed child whose fond parents proudly insist that he or she is just what you want, and give a list of the people for whom he or she has posed."[52]

Smith obviously preferred her children pure, untainted by their parents' opinions, demands, or prejudices, and this attitude wisely resulted in the naturalness of her pictures. For this naturalness, *Good Housekeeping* paid her between $1500 and $1800 per cover, a handsome sum by even today's standards of editorial payment.[53]

Her covers for this publication are certainly pleasant, and they do show children quite simply enjoying themselves, but it would be unfair to compare these works to Smith's better works, or even covers for other publications, which were often superior to those of *Good Housekeeping*. The magazine, directed at a readership of young homemakers, rarely allowed Smith to indulge in fantasy or colorful storytelling in her pictures. Part of the publication's sales philosophy was based on her creation of a child that was universally recognizable by its readership, and such children did not sit on toadstools and converse with angels.

Smith was also subject to monthly deadlines. Inspired or not, her monthly pictures had to be in hand well in advance of publication. It was not always easy to think snow in mid-June or to imagine a child picking berries when dry, naked branches were the only adornment on the local raspberry bushes. Of course Smith's file of photos of children, and a good backlog of sketches helped greatly in transcending the seasonal problems, but, even so, there are times when her lack of inspiration is seen plainly on some *Good Housekeeping* cover art.

Her less frequent covers for *Woman's Home Companion, Ladies' Home Journal,* and *Collier's,* where she was given considerably more freedom in choice of subject, often show more care and more attention to subject matter. Her Madonna-like portraits of mothers and children, seen most often on *Woman's Home Companion,* are among her most touching works, while her *Collier's* children were likely to get into predicaments that *Good Housekeeping* would never allow. One of her most touching series was the "Tragedies of Childhood," in which her *Collier's* covers blatantly displayed the horrors of a broken doll, the first haircut, a hurt finger, and being lost in a crowd of Christmas shoppers. Only the hardest heart among readers could resist the temptation to commiserate with the sad little creatures who thus learn their first hard lessons of life. Her contributions to *Collier's* included both covers and full page frontispieces, which were essentially a bonus cover, minus lettering, within the first few pages of the magazine.

In *The Ladies' Home Journal* and *Woman's Home Companion,* Smith created both original covers and adaptations of her illustrations from children's books. A

GOOD HOUSEKEEPING

SEPTEMBER, 1918   20 CENTS

Beginning
"The WEB of the SPIDER"
By Arthur Somers Roche

94. Cover, *Good House-keeping,* September, 1918

95. Cover, *Good House-keeping,* January, 1925 ▶

Good Housekeeping

35 CENTS IN CANADA

JANUARY 1925 ★

25 CENTS

DAWSON'S *New Novel* "Old Youth"

Fanny Heaslip Lea ~ *Bruce Barton* ~ *Emma-Lindsay Squier*
Frances Parkinson Keyes ~ *Konrad Bercovici* ~ *Gene Stratton-Porter*

Good Housekeeping

JUNE 1928

25 CENTS

35 CENTS IN CANADA

Beginning "Tiger, Tiger" by Honoré Willsie Morrow

Edison Marshall – Jay Gelzer – James Hopper

Herbert R. Sass – Margaret Sangster – Philip Guedalla

97. Cover, *Good House-keeping,* February, 1930 ▶

Good Housekeeping

FEBRUARY
1930

25 CENTS

Beginning "STARS AND SCISSORS"
By Mary Lawton

Margaret Kennedy — Dr. Alfred Adler — Frances P. Keyes
Coningsby Dawson — Ruth Suckow — Mary Singer

Good Housekeeping

AUGUST, 1931.   25 CENTS

FRAU ALBERT EINSTEIN —
Irvin S. Cobb — *Zona Gale* | You Lucky
Princess Der Ling | Americans !

98. Cover, *Good House-
keeping,* August, 1931

99. Cover, *Good House-
keeping,* March, 1932

particularly charming series created for the Journal concerned important firsts in the life of a child, everything from the first lesson to the first punishment. These were early works, most published just after 1900, and they still bear many of the characteristics that would vanish from her cover art as it changed over the years. Her use of pattern and decoration was strong, an important element in the picture. Usually printed in one or two colors, Smith had to concentrate on features that would make her monotonal picture more visually interesting, and she succeeded in her own fashion. Later, doing full color covers for *Good Housekeeping,* she dispensed with excessive decoration, concentrating instead on broad color forms and dramatic color contrasts for visual effect. She worked in pastels and oil paints during this later period, but few of these works match the precision and decorative impact of her early cover art in charcoal. Smith's covers show clearly her change in technique from 1900 to 1925, but even her later works, despite their refinement, capture an image of the American child that has never been repeated. Her output is totally unique, representing the various forms of childhood at various years in our history. Her children are a history lesson we enjoy learning repeatedly.

5·The Investigative Illustrator
Magazine Illustrations

HOSE who find a discomforting similarity in Smith's magazine cover art need only examine her work that appeared between the covers for insight into her versatility. While children were always her primary interest, she considered them in several ways in her "magazine studies". In a light vein she did justice to Jack and Jill and Little Miss Muffet, among others, while in a more serious approach, she examined the day-care centers of New York and the injustice of child labor in the mills of New England.

Her earliest magazine work appeared in *St. Nicholas,* the magazine for children, a publication which was heavily stocked with poems, fairy tales, and little line drawings designed to delight young minds. Smith was fortunate that this early forum for her work was available because the general circulation, adult interest publications relied almost exclusively on established professional illustrators.

Magazines for children first appeared in 1865, when *Our Young Folks* was published by the *Atlantic Monthly*. It was quickly followed by a competitor, *St. Nicholas,* which was founded by Scribner and Company. *St. Nicholas* became so popular so fast that *Our Young Folks* could not maintain the competition and was eventually bought up by the latter. In 1879 Harper Brothers, seeing that the children's market was a lucrative one, began *Harper's Young People* which changed its name to *Harper's Round Table* in 1894. Directed at the older child, the publication was filled with boys' adventure tales and current events of interest, a kind of junior version of the adult *Harper's Weekly* and *Monthly*.

Had Smith chosen to devote herself exclusively to a career as an illustrator for children's magazines, she could well have done so but one major disadvantage was payment, which was much lower than that offered by the adult publications.

It would seem that Smith had few options, however, since her choice of subject matter had little place in the adult publications of the day, *Scribner's, Century, Appleton's,* and others. These were general interest publications with lengthy articles on a variety of subjects: safaris in Africa, candle-making at home, the newest world exposition, and a general assortment of subjects designed to appeal to several adult tastes. Also included was a handsome assortment of fiction, and here is where Smith found her best outlet, although she was

Dorothy. Dorcas and
Dill
Each has been told to
sit still.
"Do not peep
Around to see
If others behave
As well as thee.
But fold thy hands
Upon thy knee
And be as good
As good can be."

not always obliged to paint children and mothers. Of course she certainly preferred such subjects and, when possible, accepted assignments in which her children could be featured. But when we look at the rare works which include subjects other than toddlers, we find that Smith also had a sound grasp of other artistic areas. For example, the illustration of the young Union soldier in "The Emigrant East," a story from the December, 1900, *Scribner's*, is interestingly composed, designed to get the viewer's attention. And who could be more paternal or scholarly than the pipe-smoking figure seen in "A Princess Listens," from the March, 1903, issue of *Frank Leslie's Popular Monthly Magazine.*

Such masculine portraits, though well executed, are infrequent; but they reaffirm Smith's prodigious talent for illustration. Those who may object to the frequent children's portraits seen in her works, saying she could do little else, may broaden their vision by examining works that show how exceedingly well she could go into other directions.

Smith's early work for *Scribner's, Century,* and *Collier's* had a reportorial flavor and simple charm. In December, 1902, *Century* featured her illustrations to accompany a lengthy article called, "While the Mother Works: A Look at the Day Nurseries of New York" by Lillie Hamilton French. Smith traveled to various day nurseries throughout New York City to research the illustrations which show a day in the life of day-care youngsters. They are seen lining up for a

100. "Dorothy, Dorcas, and Dill," from *St. Nicholas,* May, 1891

101. Cover, *Good House- ▶ keeping,* July, 1926

Good Housekeeping

JULY 1926

25 CENTS

35 CENTS IN CANADA

JESSIE WILLCOX SMITH

"The Purple Scarf" *by Fanny Heaslip Lea*

Juliet Wilbor Tompkins—James Hopper—Frances P. Keyes
Margaret Widdemer—Emily Newell Blair—Herbert R. Sass

Good Housekeeping

JANUARY 1930

25 CENTS
35 CENTS IN CANADA

1930

Beginning a NEW NOVEL by the Author of "THE CONSTANT NYMPH"

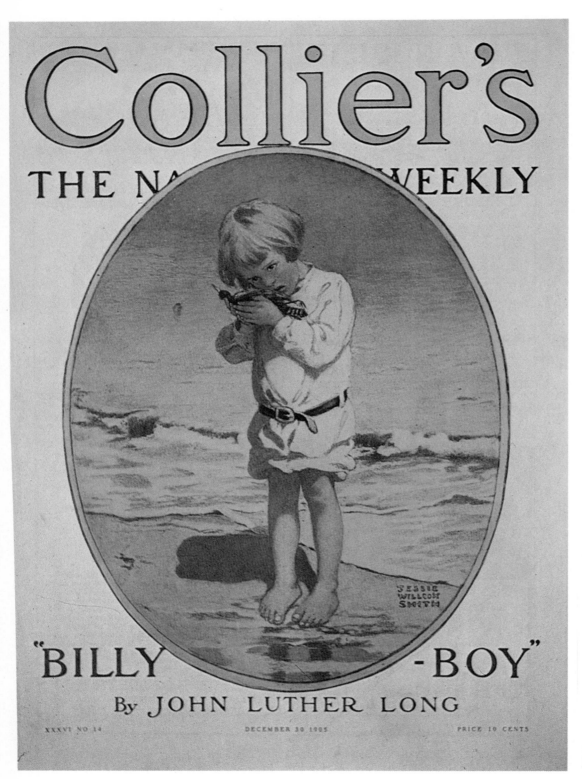

Collier's
THE NA... WEEKLY

"BILLY -BOY"
By JOHN LUTHER LONG

XXXVI NO 14   DECEMBER 30 1905   PRICE 10 CENTS

104. Cover, *Collier's,*
December 30, 1905

The Christmas Present Number

WOMAN'S HOME COMPANION

DECEMBER 1913   FIFTEEN CENTS

THE CROWELL PUBLISHING COMPANY

105. Cover, *Woman's Home Companion*, December, 1913

THE LADIES' HOME JOURNAL

NOVEMBER 1912   FIFTEEN CENTS

THE CURTIS PUBLISHING COMPANY PHILADELPHIA

106. Cover, *The Ladies'
Home Journal,*
November, 1912

107. "Cinderella,"
*Woman's Home
Companion,* September,
1913

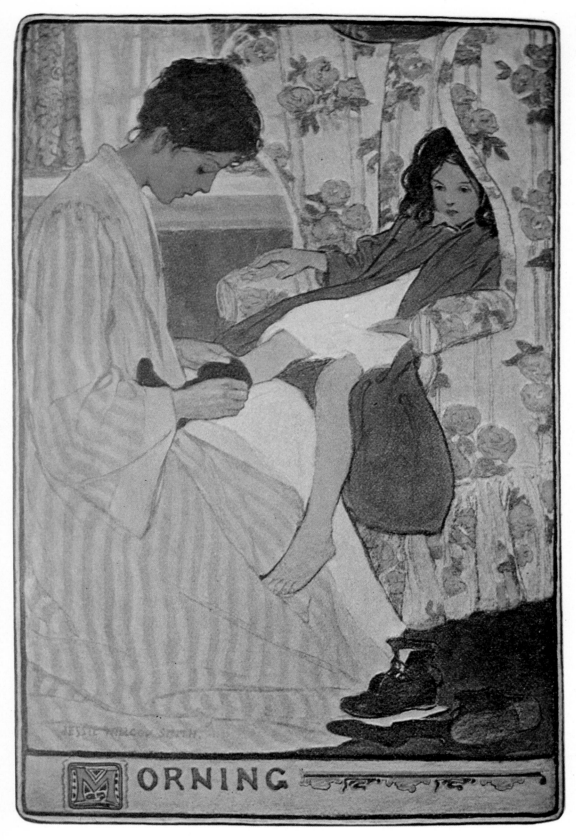

MORNING

108. "Morning" from "A Mother's Days," *Scribner's*, December, 1902

FAIRY TALES

JESSIE WILLCOX SMITH.

The Garden Wall

110. "The Garden Wall,"
from "The Child in the
Garden," *Scribner's*,
December, 1903

111. "The Green Door,"
from "The Child in the
Garden," *Scribner's*,
December, 1903

112. "Caught in the
Act," from *Collier's*,
December 12, 1909

113. "Goldilocks,"
*Woman's Home
Companion,* October,
1913

114. "Goldilocks and
the Three Bears,"
Collier's

115. "Let Dogs Delight ▶
to Bark and Bite,"
*Woman's Home
Companion*

face washing at 8 A.M., standing on a rooftop playground, and taking an afternoon nap. In these sensitive, touching illustrations, Smith used charcoal and pencil with the softest possible shadings to capture images of child day care.

A less reportorial group of illustrations, although of interest, was done for "Kitchen Sketches," by Elizabeth Hale Gilman, seen in the May, 1903, *Scribner's*. These two color works, drawn in charcoals and pastel orange or yellow to indicate the glow of a cooking flame or sunlight coming in a window, followed young homemakers through their daily cooking chores. The works could not be simpler in their feeling, yet they are totally captivating. Similarly, Smith's illustrations for Gilman's "Home Sketches," which appeared in the March, 1904, *Scribner's,* are equally charming. An illustration of a young woman on a horse is elegantly drawn and reflective of a peaceful moment.

Obviously, Smith did not need children to make a successful picture, but she preferred to include them in her works. As her children began to appeal to more readers, they became a staple of her output. The magazine editors and publishers realized soon enough that Smith was at her best when drawing children, and recognizing the appeal these drawings had for adults, they quickly joined with her in developing themes and subjects that would include children.

Smith's entry into the highly competitive world of adult magazine illustration

came quickly after she began her studies with Howard Pyle. He helped her find her early assignments, and by 1900 she was established firmly with *Collier's, Harper's, Scribner's,* and other adult market publications. One remarkable aspect of Smith's illustration for such publications is that her works are often seen alone without accompanying text. It was thought that her works had enough of a following to stand on their own. Few artists achieved the same privilege, among them are Maxfield Parrish, Jules Guerin, J. C. Leyendecker, and a handful of others.

Among these early series illustrations, accompanied by only a small poem written to highlight the illustrations, were "A Mother's Days," appearing in the December, 1902, *Scribner's;* "A Child's World," from the December, 1909, *McClure's;* and "The Child in a Garden," seen in the December, 1903, *Scribner's.* It is no accident that these color series works appeared in December issues. They were, after all, Christmas gifts to the readers, gifts that would perhaps guarantee continued readerships and subscriptions.

Smith preferred to work in oil, adding color to previously done charcoal sketches. This combination of media gives these early works a soft, pastel-like quality, in which the grain of the paper and other textures are an important element of the picture. "A Mother's Days" follows several young mothers through their daily relationships with their young children. Dressing the child, playing in the garden, playing checkers, eating supper; and going to bed were the features of her young mothers' days. The works, which show the women with one or two young children, are rich with the strong elements so important to Smith's early work: repeated use of pattern, backlighting and other unconventional lighting patterns, and sentimental, touching moments of affection.

"The Child in a Garden" follows two children through the gardens of

118. Illustration from "The Emigrant East," *Scribner's* December, 1900

119. "Supper," from "A Mother's Days," *Scribner's.* December, 1902

(162)

SUPPER.

120. "No one could tell
what flowers they
were," from "A
Princess Listens,"
*Frank Leslie's Popular
Monthly,* March, 1903

21. "The Creche,
Halsey Nursery," from
'While the Mother
Works," *Century*,
December, 1902

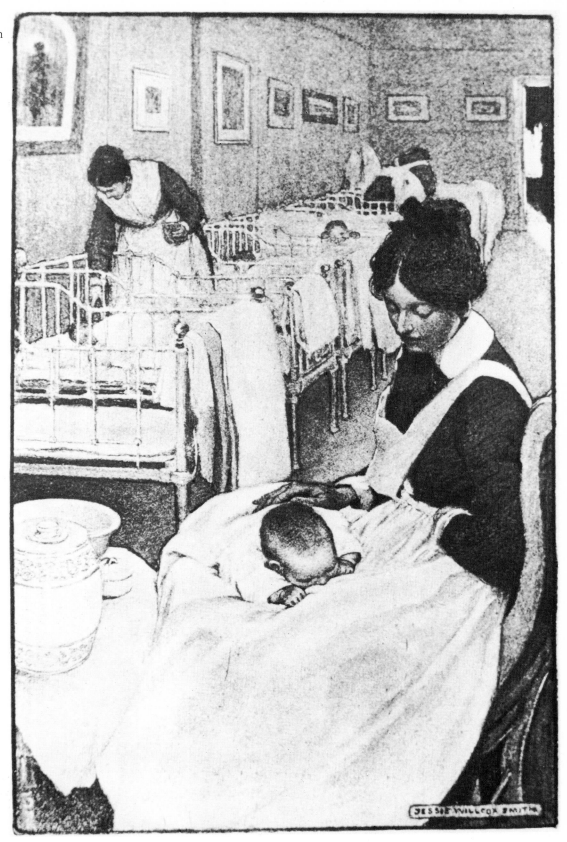

Cogslea, a verdant landscape in which children's fantasies come miraculously to life. "A Child's World" from the December, 1909, *McClure's,* is a later series on this same theme which follows children through forest and garden alike, exploring and discovering the mysteries that are common to every young adventurer.

Another colorful, appealing series was "The Five Senses," from the October, 1907, *McClure's,* in which children were shown experiencing hearing (in a conch shell at the beach), touching, tasting, seeing, and smelling. Accompanied by poems by Angela M. Keyes, the series was published in book form in 1911.

Smith worked exceptionally well in this series format, but she also provided individual illustrations for publications, which would use them as a decorative centerfold or as a frontispiece. An early edition of *Harper's Bazar* features such a double page illustration, "The Story Hour," which depicts a young mother telling a story to three of her children. Smith cleverly makes the pictures more human by employing a technique she would use again in other pictures. The girl on the far right of the picture looks dreamily in the direction of the viewer, as if she has taken her thoughts away from her mother's story and is suddenly distracted by the presence of an outsider. One can easily relate to the reality of an inattentive child, and Smith has thus brought the viewer into the picture after he or she locks eyes with the distracted little girl.

In *Collier's,* Smith's frequent frontispieces were a popular weekly addition. Her illustrations for this publication dealt most often with the harsh realities and wondrous pleasures of growing up. Illustrations like "Kept In," which show an unhappy young scholar who is being punished for misbehaving in class and "The Recitation," which recalls a moment of terror in early school life, were neatly balanced by "Autumn Days" and other more pleasant memories of childhood.

Collier's was among the most lucrative projects available to Smith in the early 1900s, but the publication made demands that were difficult to keep. Like the other illustrators A. B. Frost, Charles Dana Gibson, E. W. Kemble, Frederick Remington and F. X. Leyendecker, Smith agreed to a two-year exclusive contract with *Collier's Weekly.* Her contract, which lasted from May 1, 1904, to April 30, 1906, was engaged despite the objections of Violet Oakley, who felt it restricted her friend during an important period of growth and building her relationships with other publications. *Collier's* itself published a statement which explained to its readers what "exclusivity" meant: "To draw 'exclusively' for *Collier's* means to an artist the opportunity to do less work and better work, to be free from the grind of magazine illustration, to have a freer hand, a larger space, a more important subject."[54]

Oakley had different thoughts on the matter. After Smith had signed the contract without her knowledge while she was in Harrisburg, working on her Pennsylvania State Capitol commission, Oakley called her friend's decision "reprehensible."[55] Smith did not always follow her friend's business advice, but after a time, she did begin to see Oakley's point of view. Her contract, while freeing her from scattered small projects for numerous publications, also

122. "As a special privilege, the zealot bore it in blazing," from "Kitchen Sketches," *Scribner's* May, 1903

(166)

AS A SPECIAL PRIVILEGE THE ZEALOT BORE IT IN BLAZING.

JESSIE WILLCOX SMITH.

123. " 'Good day, little bird, good day,' " from "Within the Ring of Singing," *Frank Leslie's Popular Monthly,* August, 1903

124. "She rode up on ▶ old white Bunny," from "Home Sketches," *Scribner's,* March, 1904

prevented her from doing work that she wanted to do for other publishers. In a lengthy exchange of letters to Underwood Johnson, publisher of *Century*, she turned down an earlier spoken commitment to do an illustrated article on the Red Rose Inn. Smith would have enjoyed doing the feature, and she attempted to obtain permission from *Collier's* for this one digression from her contract, but the publication refused, and the article never appeared.[56]

125. "She began to mount the stairs which led to the upper floor," from "In the Closed Room," *McClure's* August, 1904

126. "The First Lesson," ▶
The Ladies' Home Journal
December, 1904

The First Lesson

127. "Hearing," "The Five Senses," *McClure's*, October, 1907

This was not the only project that had to be shelved and which was eventually lost as a result of her tight contract. Smith had wanted to do a series called "The Spoiling of the American Child," and she offered it to *Collier's,* but the publication was worried about the series' negative connotations and refused it. Smith still believed in her idea, but she could take it to no one else, and she let it pass until another time, a time which, of course, never came.

Once her contract had expired, Smith returned to supplying work for other publications, although she still continued to do work for *Collier's.* In 1908, she began a major series for the *Ladies' Home Journal* which found its way into book form during the next year. "The Seven Ages of Childhood," a superb series of illustrations for poems by Carolyn Wells, showed the progression of a child from infancy to young motherhood. Illustrated in mixed media, the works appeared only in black and white in the magazine, but were printed in full color in the book.

"The Seven Ages of Childhood" represented a trend that would repeat itself

128. "First the Infant ▶ in its Mother's Arms," from "The Seven Ages of Childhood," *The Ladies' Home Journal,* November, 1908

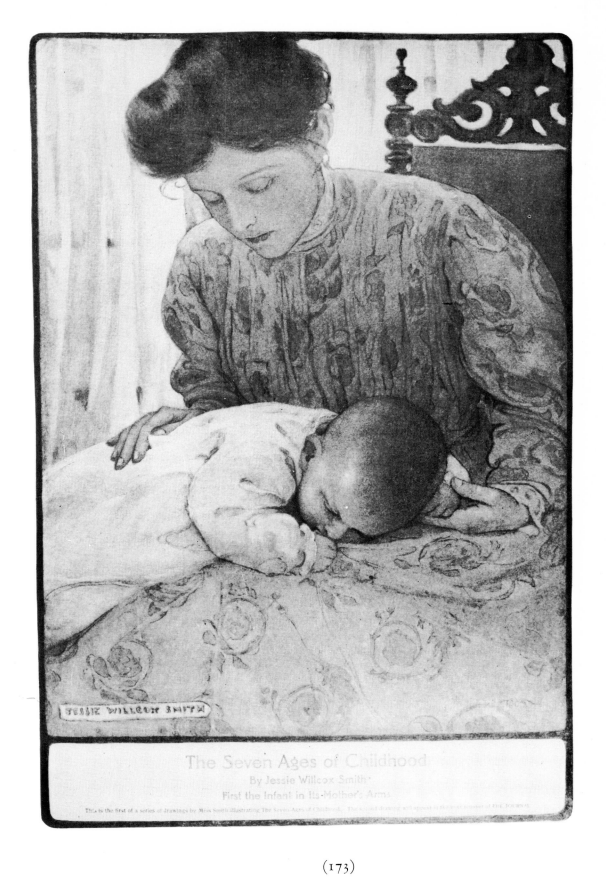

JESSIE WILLCOX SMITH

The Seven Ages of Childhood
By Jessie Willcox Smith
First the Infant in Its Mother's Arms

This is the first of a series of drawings by Miss Smith illustrating The Seven Ages of Childhood. The second drawing will appear in the next number of THE JOURNAL.

The Seven Ages of Childhood

By Jessie Willcox Smith

Then the Toddling Baby Boy, With Shining Morning Face, Creeping Like Snail

This is the second of a series of drawings by Miss Smith illustrating The Seven Ages of Childhood. The third drawing will appear in the next number of THE JOURNAL

129. "Then the Toddling Baby Boy, With Shining Morning Face, Creeping Like a Snail," from "The Seven Ages of Childhood," *The Ladies' Home Journal*, December 1908

The Seven Ages of Childhood
By Jessie Willcox Smith
Then the Scholar, With Eyes Severe and Hair of Formal Cut

This is the fifth of a series of drawings by Miss Smith, illustrating The Seven Ages of Childhood. The sixth will appear in an early number of THE JOURNAL.

130. "Then the Scholar with Eyes Severe and Hair of Formal Cut," from "The Seven Ages of Childhood," *The Ladies' Home Journal,* April, 1909

131. "Then the Lean and Thoughtful Maiden, with Dreaming Eyes and Quiet Mien," from "The Seven Ages of Childhood," *The Ladies' Home Journal,* August, 1909.

throughout Smith's career. Whenever possible, she would obtain rights to reprint her magazine illustrations in book form. Among her most popular series for magazines and in books was "Dickens' Children," which featured four drawings in the December, 1911, *Scribner's,* and two additional works in the August, 1912, issue. Among the Charles Dickens characters who were interpreted by Smith were Tiny Tim from *A Christmas Carol,* David Copperfield, Pip from *Great Expectations,* and other youthful citizens of the English master

132. "Hansel and Gretel," *Collier's,* April, 1913

133. "The North Wind
Doth Blow," Campbell   (178)
Prints, 1915

134. "The Goose Girl,"
Duffield and Company,
1911

Painted by Jessie Wilcox Smith for Cream of Wheat Company.   Copyright 1909 by Cream of Wheat Company.

"I KNOW THAT MAN"

137. "I Know that
Man," advertisement,
The Cream of Wheat
Company, 1909

(182)

138. Advertisement,
Campbell's Soup
Company, 1928

139. Poster, Interchurch
World Movement, 1919

140. Poster, American
Red Cross, 1918

CHILDREN'S BOOK WEEK
NOVEMBER 10th to 15th 1919

MORE BOOKS IN THE HOME!

142. Portrait, Corning J. ▶
Pearson, 1918, oil,
20″ x 25″

141. Poster, American
Library Association,
1919

CORNING

JESSIE WILLCOX SMITH.

143. Portrait, Olive
Pearson, 1922, oil,
31″ x 50″

144. Portrait, Jeanne C. ►
Flood, 1929, oil,
18″ x 24″

(188)

146. Portrait, Francis ▶
McIlhenny, 1915, oil,
36″ x 49″

145. Portrait, Eleanor,
1915, watercolor,
24″ x 30″

147. Portrait, Ann and
Mary Leisenring, 1922,
oil, 39″ x 50″

author's works. In 1912, in a special arrangement, *Scribner's* published the works in book form, paying Smith an additional royalty. In 1925, these illustrations were resurrected again for another volume published by *Scribner's* called, *The Children of Dickens*, which featured synopses of the author's works.

Ironically, despite their enthusiastic acceptance by the reading public, Smith was dissatisfied with her Dickens paintings. Writing to Underwood Johnson, publisher of *Century*, who had written to Smith after the series appeared in *Scribner's*, asking her to do a similar interpretation for *Century*, she explained, "Your note has done me a world of good. I have been feeling very blue about my Dickens pictures. Mr. Chupier had great difficulty with the reproductions as the men went on strike while these pictures were in the works, and he was obliged, as he said, 'to take anything.' But the result was a bitter disappointment to me, and that I know that you will find good in them is balm to my wounds."[57]

After another exchange in which Smith and Johnson tried to develop an interesting series, they decided on the children of Rudyard Kipling, another English author who had captured American public attentions. After several months of work, Smith at last submitted the works to Johnson, but her accompanying letter was almost apologetic in nature, as if she knew he would refuse them.

I do hope you will find in them the appeal for book form. I have certainly tried to put into them all that I felt – though perhaps no children are quite

Pease porridge hot, pease porridge cold.
Pease porridge in the pot nine days old.

148. "Pease Porridge
Hot," *Good House-
keeping,* December, 1912

as appealing as Dickens', Kipling's are a totally different type – so brave and manly – but of course their appeal should be in a different way. I hope I have shown it. I am so sorry that the black and white drawings were disappointing – the child in them had perhaps outgrown the appealing age. Send the Kiplings back if you don't like them – but of course I hope you will.[58]

149. "Rain, Rain, Go Away," *Good Housekeeping*, April, 1913

The expected rejection arrived in short order with detailed instructions on how the pictures should be changed. Smith found the changes extensive and impossible to make without completely altering the character of the illustrations, and she replied, perhaps with some sarcasm, "I surely do not want anything to appear in *The Century* from me that was not, in your opinion, my best."[59] She refused to change the works, and when Johnson suggested printing them in black and white instead of color, she would not hear of it. She stood firmly by the integrity of her works, willing to accept reasonable changes but unwilling to make major alterations. She wrote of one of the Kipling illustrations, "The interest in 'The Bushwood Boy' is in the experiences of the children in a *dream country,* and to show the children large with very little country (as it would there have to be) would do away with the dream quality and make it like any other picture. And I particularly want that one for some future time, provided of course you want to take chances on an uncertain quantity like myself!"[60]

"Kipling's Children" were eventually published in *Scribner's,* but they never appeared as a separate entity in book form. Smith did, however, use some of the illustrations in later books which combined children's stories from disparate sources.

During the period prior to the First World War, Smith began a series of illustrated nursery rhymes for *Good Housekeeping Magazine,* which included such storybook notables as Jack and Jill, Little Jack Horner, Peter, Peter Pumpkin Eater, and other nursery rhyme greats. *Woman's Home Companion,* on the other hand, featured a series of color illustrations of her visualizations of Goldilocks, Hansel and Gretel, Jack and the Beanstalk, and other children's fairy tales. In virtually every case, her magazine illustrations done during this period were again reproduced in book form, a fact that contributed greatly to her income from illustrations.

Undoubtedly, Smith was a consistent presence in the magazines of the early 1900s. She reached more viewers than any artist whose works were displayed in galleries or museums. The art critic Rilla Evelyn Jackman, writing in *American Arts* in 1929, summed up Jessie Willcox Smith's contribution to the American illustration scene in one neat, appropriate paragraph: "In the peculiar place which Miss Smith holds in the art world she is quite as worthy of our interest as are many of the artists who paint easel pictures for our great exhibitions or murals for our public buildings. In fact, she, more than most of them, is bringing art to the people. We are proud of the eagle, and fond of the warbler, but even for them we would not give up the robin and the bluebird."[61]

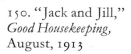

150. "Jack and Jill," *Good Housekeeping,* August, 1913

6·From Soap to Soup
Advertisements

F all the activities she performed for publications, Smith found least satisfaction in advertising. Advertisers, unlike magazine editors who looked for a particular style and type of subject for a cover, were more demanding. Every aspect of an advertisement was subject to review and revision. But like most illustrators who did advertising art, Smith realized that advertisers paid well for the privilege of instructing their artists.

Early in their careers, when advertising illustration was an aspect of Pyle's teaching, both Smith and Green complained to him about the many advertisements they had to do for *The Ladies' Home Journal*. His response was, "I can only say to you to do advertisement illustration for that magazine you don't altogether care for, as if they were full page illustrations for *Harper's*. I can think of no surer method of securing eventually the latter."[62]

It was advice well taken. During the years just after her work with Pyle, Smith began a series of Ivory Soap advertisements for Procter and Gamble. Usually featuring a mother bathing a youngster or children at play, her Ivory advertisements appeared in *Pictorial Review, Woman's Home Companion, Youth's Companion, Harper's Weekly,* and, of course, *Collier's.* What a likely partnership: the purity of Ivory Soap and the innocent Jessie Willcox Smith child.

Smith had already drawn dozens of unsigned ads for *The Ladies' Home Journal,* which one critic called "a school in which to learn the limitations of reproductive work."[63] One of these works, for Cuticura Soap, shows the uninspired classical costume art drawn while she was at the Academy. Smith obviously put some of her early training to convenient use in her Journal advertisements.

Kodak was another early advertiser who took advantage of Smith's talent. While it may seem contradictory for a camera and film manufacturer to advertise its products with illustrations, and not photos, company executives knew that a greater public response would be elicited from a combination advertising campaign: drawings one month and photos the next. Smith's delicate studies of ordinary families with new cameras were no doubt responsible for bringing the early box-camera into thousands of homes.

Though she did not particularly enjoy doing advertising art, Smith could not deny that it was lucrative. Edith Emerson related a story that occurred at

"Disfigured for Life"

Is the despairing cry of thousands afflicted
  with unsightly skin diseases.
Do you realize what this disfiguration
  means to sensitive souls?
It means isolation, seclusion.
It is a bar to social and business success.
Do you wonder that despair seizes upon
  these sufferers when
Doctors fail, standard remedies fail,
And nostrums prove worse than useless?
Skin diseases are most obstinate to cure or
  even relieve.
It is an easy matter to claim to cure them,
  but quite another thing to do so.
CUTICURA REMEDIES
Have earned the right to be called Skin
  Specifics,
Because for years they have met with most
  remarkable success.
There are cases that they cannot cure, but
  they are few indeed.
It is no long-drawn-out, expensive experi-
  ment.
25c. invested in a cake of
CUTICURA SOAP
Will prove more convincing than a page
  of advertisement.
In short
CUTICURA WORKS WONDERS,
And its cures are simply marvelous.
Now is the time
To take CUTICURA.
CURES made in WINTER
Are permanent.

Sold throughout the world. Price, Cuti-
cura, 50c.; Soap, 25c.; Resolvent, $1.00.
Potter Drug and Chemical Corporation,
Sole Proprietors, Boston. "All About the
Skin, Scalp, and Hair" mailed free.

151. Advertisement for Cuticura Soap, one of Smith's early works for *The Ladies' Home Journal*

Cogslea while Violet Oakley was at work on the Pennsylvania capitol commission. Oakley had spent considerable time on her murals, earning $20,000 but this sum was divided over a four year period, and her dedication to the Harrisburg assignment left Oakley with little time for other work. Consequently, near the end of the project, her finances were seriously low. She had been troubled by financial problems for weeks, but she was too proud to ask for help from any of the others. One morning Smith called her friend into her studio and quietly handed her a check for $1000, refusing to let her return it. Touched and grateful, she began to cry. To calm her, Smith smiled and said, "That's all right, Violet. I can do an Ivory soap ad anytime and make that up right away."[64]

Smith did not always create advertising illustrations for monetary gain, and when she contributed her talents to organizations like the Red Cross or the Philadelphia Welfare Federation, her works were less commercial and more sincere. One such example remains from the First World War, when the United States Committee on Public Information asked the artist Charles Dana Gibson to form a Division of Pictorial Publicity, an organization of professional illustrators who donated their time and talent to create posters, cartoons, and newspaper advertisements for 58 different government agencies. Smith was asked to do a poster to help raise funds for a Christmas campaign for the Red

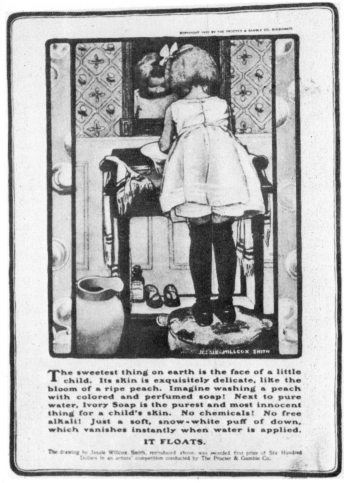

152. Advertisement,
Ivory Soap, 1901

153. Advertisement,
Ivory Soap, 1902

Cross. Her work, which shows a small boy pasting a Red Cross flag in a window below a Christmas wreath, is one of the best known posters of the period. The nature of the poster seems to show Smith's delight in creating the image. The carefully attentive youngster works hard at getting the service flag straight, and this simple image is offset nicely by the colorful patterned curtains which frame the scene. The poster was popular, and it was also used by the Red Cross on the cover of an issue of its monthly magazine.

The following year, as part of a promotion to encourage the reading of books by children, Smith designed a poster called "More Books in the Home" for the National Association of Book Publishers which promoted a Library Week campaign from November 10 to 15, 1919. Unlike the Red Cross poster, which was printed in hundreds of thousands of copies, as were most war posters of the time, the Library Week poster emerged only in a small edition and is therefore considered a collector's item among today's Smith aficionados.

Smith was never really active as a poster artist, although she did freely con-

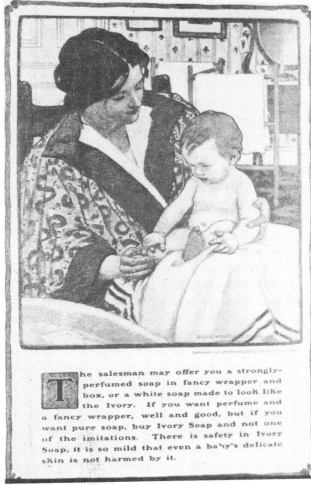

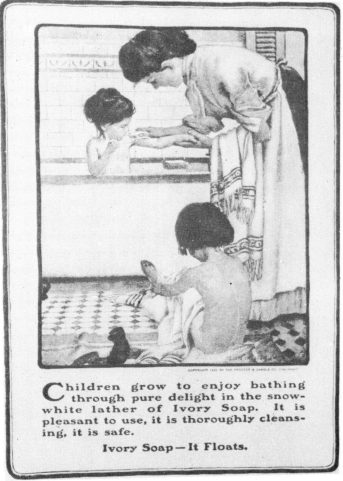

The salesman may offer you a strongly-perfumed soap in fancy wrapper and box, or a white soap made to look like the Ivory. If you want perfume and a fancy wrapper, well and good, but if you want pure soap, buy Ivory Soap and not one of the imitations. There is safety in Ivory Soap, it is so mild that even a baby's delicate skin is not harmed by it.

Children grow to enjoy bathing through pure delight in the snow-white lather of Ivory Soap. It is pleasant to use, it is thoroughly cleansing, it is safe.

Ivory Soap—It Floats.

154. Advertisement,
Ivory Soap, 1901

155. Advertisement,
Ivory Soap, 1902

tribute her time for philanthropic goals. When her series, "The Child in the Garden" was published in *Scribner's* magazine, the publication printed blow-ups of the illustrations in poster form to advertise the issue, but these are not posters in the purest sense, having been used as illustrations first.

After the War, when Smith's *Good Housekeeping* covers and her illustrated books had developed their large followings, Smith was approached by many advertisers for work. She did not accept all jobs since she was too busy with her other work, but occasional advertisements for Campbell's Soup, Fleischmann's Yeast, and other firms do appear in publications from 1918 to the mid-1920s.

One unusual advertisement was drawn in 1924 when the Standard Sanitary Manufacturing Company, a maker of bathtubs and other bathroom furnishings, began an advertisement campaign. Using 84 models and a professional photographer, the firm took 150 poses they felt would best suit the firm's image. Artists were then selected and given the photographs to interpret in their own style. Smith receive an image of a little girl climbing into a bathtub, and her

Before the days of Ivory Soap, it was a very
serious matter to soil one's dainty frock.
But now —

*"Ivory Soap and water will not injure
anything that water, alone, will not harm."*

IVORY SOAP · · · · · 99 44/100% PURE

THOUGH the children sometimes wash each other with greater vigor than care,
their tender skins are not chafed if Ivory Soap is used.

Ivory Soap can be rubbed into the most delicate skin thoroughly and continually without causing the slightest irritation. It is free from uncombined alkali and from every
other material that has an injurious, or even questionable, effect.

Choice ingredients and exact manufacturing processes give to Ivory Soap the distinctive
mildness that makes it as harmless and as grateful to every skin as pure, clear, soft water.

IVORY SOAP · · · · · 99 44/100% PURE

156. Advertisement,
Ivory Soap, 1914

157. Advertisement,
Ivory Soap, 1917

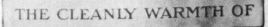

158. Advertisement,
American Radiator
Company, 1915

159. Poster, The
Philadelphia Welfare
Federation, 1926

resulting drawing was considered so successful by the company's executives
that it was reproduced in color in several leading publications.[65]

Smith's advertising activities diminished during her later years when she
devoted more of her time to the covers of *Good Housekeeping* and to her portraits.
It must be admitted, however, that her appealing youngsters, whether washing
their dolls' faces or devouring bowls of soup, did more for the cause of com-
merce than most of the other advertising illustrations of her time.

7· Portrait of the Child
Philadelphia's Youth

WHEN a large selection of Jessie Willcox Smith's portraits of children were shown at a December, 1924 exhibit of her work at the Philadelphia Art Alliance, Edith Emerson wrote in the Introduction to the catalog that Smith's portrait painting style was "in the English tradition, established in the United States by Copley, Stuart, and West. It is well-mannered, clean, and graceful, and a generous dash of common sense gives it savor and freshness."[66]

There was indeed an English flavor to her portraits which were meant to grace the parlors and dens of some of Philadelphia's most opulent homes. Her young subjects possessed names that were automatically associated with wealth, reserve, and good breeding. Leisenring, McIlhenny, Spalding, Houston, and others were names not unknown to Philadelphia Society. They were the names of bankers, industrialists, and prominent landowners. Unlike the children seen on her *Good Housekeeping* covers or in the pages of her illustrated books, these young models were posed in a manner becoming the association with their names. If posed in a garden, her subjects were never seen climbing a wall to reach a distant rose. They instead stood quietly nearby, admiring its delicacy. Her seated models, who may have fidgeted nervously while impatiently posing for her knowledgeable brush, appear to have been angelically calm, a stuffed toy animal held at the side or a picture book on the lap.

Smith was too professional to be overly troubled by a restless or nervous child. In her warm and spacious studio, she kept a ready reserve of tea, milk, and cookies, nutrient enticements designed to keep the child still while she quickly sketched the beginnings of a picture. She herself recounted another method for keeping a child's attention:

> The way I do it is to tell fairy stories – tell them with great animation! A child will always look directly at anyone who is telling a story; so while I paint, I tell tales marvelous to hear. But to paint with half one's mind, and tell a thrilling, eye-opening tale with the other half is an art I have not fully conquered even yet. Alas the resplendent Cinderella sometimes stops halfway down the stairs, slipper and all, while I am considering the subtle curve in the outline of the listener's charming, enthralled little face.[67]

The artist's quick eye and her thorough knowledge of the child's proportions

160. Portrait of Eleanor,
1913, oil, 16″ x 19″

kept her from being disturbed while children played or chattered away as she painted.

One of her most valuable tools as a portrait painter was the camera. Her earliest photographs, taken while she was still in the Chestnut Street studio, were stiff portraits of classically-clad ladies, a series of pictures which echoed the plaster statues at the Academy. By the First World War Smith had developed her photographic talents if not into a fine art at least to a useful method by which to capture those fleeting moments of childhood perfection that would later be transformed into innocence on canvas. A photograph of Jeanne C. Flood, taken by Smith prior to a portrait session, clearly illustrates how much of the photograph was later recaptured in the portrait.

During the summer months, Smith let her future portrait subjects wander in

the plush gardens at Cogslea or Cogshill while she snapped photographs of the children with her Kodak box camera. Smith's intent in photography was never to duplicate the photographic image in oil. She referred to her photographs only occasionally, and when she did they were strictly a reference to positioning, props, and settings. The latter were especially important to the artist, who once wrote:

> Many of my portraits are painted out-of-doors. Out-of-doors seems the natural background for childhood. Given leaves, and flowers and sunshine, which is theirs by right, their little faces glow in the full light as though illumed from within. Heavy draperies and dark shadows, with the strong concentrated studio light, are not expressive of childhood to me. I want children under the blue sky, in the shining radiance and joy which is their

birthright, and with the flowers of God's earth, of which they are only a higher bloom at their feet.[68]

One would think, from such rosy published commentaries, that the children she painted were as peaceful as snowflakes, and that she treated them with the appropriate gentility. In truth, Smith was never sentimental about her young subjects. An ill-mannered, noisy child did not please her, though she admitted that they "are often like this, poor little things, through no fault of their own."[69]

Most people who posed for her as children, people who no doubt were well-behaved models, recall an atmosphere of grace and charm. They remember a

162. Portrait of Isabel Lewis, 1916, oil, 18″ x 26″

stately woman who was patient and pleasant, sometimes telling stories, but who most often sat quietly and intently at work.

Smith's greatest problem as a portrait painter came not from the children but from their parents. "Where are her dimples? She has such beautiful dimples." "That's not my Charlie's chin – it's much too long." "Why she never sits in that position. That's not my little girl!"

Such statements, a headache for any portrait painter, did little to endear the parents to Smith, but she accepted them as an occupational hazard. Smith did her best to understand the desires of the parents before a portrait was contracted and begun, consulting with them at great length about the pose, costume, background, types of accessories, and the ultimate expression on the child's face. All her consultations, however, were at times to little avail. One mother who asked that her child – a restless little chatterbox – be painted in a serene pose complained that the finished portrait did not capture her little girl's mouth in true fashion. "How could I," snapped back Smith, "she never had it shut."[70]

Though it was difficult and annoying, Smith would make reasonable changes to suit the parents, feeling many times that the portraits could take some alteration without irreparable harm to the final quality of the work. But one portrait required so many parent-demanded changes that Smith finally refused to make them, keeping the work herself, displaying it defiantly for years in her own studio.

Edith Emerson, a close ally who had seen first-hand the nervous state to which some overbearing parents could bring Smith, came to her friend's defense in an article written in conjunction with an exhibit of Smith's portraits at the Philadelphia Art Alliance in the summer of 1925:

> There is a time in the career of every portrait when its life hangs by a thread . . . Families of sitters would do well to memorize the ancient proverb about 'too many cooks,' for lack of technical training seldom puts the soft pedal on opinions. There may be persons who would hesitate to mix up chemicals whose constituent properties were unknown to them, yet they cheerfully cause explosions among the ingredients of a picture, because they are harboring photographic standards in their minds. Every sincere portrait painter recognizes the necessity for truthful presentation of the character of his model, but on far too many occasions psychological cross currents force the greater truth to be sacrificed to the lesser. The ability to cooperate in any enterprise without hindering its orderly progress is a fine art in itself.[71]

Smith herself could never have publicly expressed those sentiments because portrait work represented a fair share of her income, and Chestnut Hill society was too close-knit to allow scandalous criticism of her wealthy clients. In a particularly productive year, Smith would paint over a dozen portraits, and her fees were far from modest for the time: $500 for a bust portrait, $1000 for a full-length portrait, and negotiable fees for dual or multi-child portraits.

During the First World War, Smith participated in a government sponsored

163. Alice, an early
portrait, rejected by the
child's parents and hung
in Smith's studio

program in which artists would offer free portrait commissions to citizens who purchased several thousand dollars worth of war bonds. One wealthy Philadelphian who purchased $10,000 worth of war bonds had Smith paint her three sons, "little yellow-headed fellows, all dressed in canary colored suits and as much alike as the proverbial peas."[72] One was posed in a small kiddie car, another with a toy elephant, and another with a toy camel. On the mother's instruction, Smith included the children's names as part of the portraits, a feature that would, in less artistic hands, have done irreparable damage to the work. Smith, however, made the names an integral part of each painting, a feature that, in this instance, enhances the pictures.

(207)

When working for less wealthy clients the artist would charge more moderate fees for portraits and would receive permission from the parents to use the child's picture as an illustration or magazine cover. While most main line or Chestnut Hill Philadelphians would have been horrified to find their child's picture on the cover of a mass magazine, clients with more modest incomes and backgrounds were delighted with the possibility. Smith would obtain a dual payment from the work – a significant fee from the editorial office and a more reasonable one from the parents who were the eventual recipients of the picture when the magazine had finished with it.

While editorial portraits were usually completed to meet a deadline, her commissions for private families were generally more carefully and slowly prepared. After two or three sittings of two hours' duration, Smith would work up to six months on a single commission. This work, of course, was interspersed with her numerous other activities. At any one time, the artist could have up to a dozen projects at once.

The care and interest she put into portrait work is evident in many works, especially a large picture of Ann and Mary Leisenring, described by Edith Emerson as "tiny tight rosebuds of delicious pink."[73] Positioned on a dark love seat, brought to the Smith studio by the children's parents, the two little girls are dressed in simple pink dresses, with modest pink ribbons in their hair. "Children are like flowers," Smith once said, "It seems to be inappropriate to dress them in bizarre colors or to paint them in a bizarre manner."[74]

The subtle color harmonies seen in the portrait of Molly Tyler, who lovingly caresses her pekingese puppy, is a testament to Smith's skill with oils. The child's skin is so appropriately translucent against the backdrop of foliage, and the direct attention-grabbing composition was a trademark of her better portraits. There was no mistaking her intent in this work. The child, all-important, captured forever in a pose of undeniable beauty and tenderness, appears here to be the most vital and touching subject any painter could have discovered.

Yet not every portrait was such a success. A multiple portrait of the Butcher children, set in an illustrative tea-party mode, sacrifices the character of the individual children to the accoutrements and background. A portrait of young Isabel Crowder, a lovely 16-year-old with long flaxen hair, becomes more of a study of a fashionable hat than an insightful picture of character.

Successful or not, Jessie Willcox Smith, never regretted the presence of youngsters in her studio. She lived to immortalize other people's children. She was a champion of childhood whose happiest moments came when placing a small child's personality forever on canvas or board.

"It has been one long joyous road along which troop delightful children," she wrote, "happy children, sad children, thoughtful children, and above all wondering, imaginative children, who give to their charmingly original thoughts a delicious quaintness of expression. I love to paint them all."[75]

Appendices
A· Chronology

1863 September 6. Born in Philadelphia, daughter of Charles Henry Smith and Katherine DeWitt (Willcox) Smith.

1879 Leaves Philadelphia for Cincinnati to begin study for a career as a kindergarten teacher.

1884 Returns to Philadelphia after giving up teaching to enroll in the School of Design for Women.
Studies portrait painting with William Sartain.

1885–1888 Enrolls in the Pennsylvania Academy of the Fine Arts, where she studies art under Thomas Eakins and others.

1888 Leaves the Academy to being a career as an illustrator.
May, her first published illustration appears in *St. Nicholas,* the magazine for children.
Obtains a post in the advertising department of the *Ladies' Home Journal.*

1894 Howard Pyle begins his Saturday afternoon illustration class at Drexel Institute, and Smith enrolls.

1895 Elizabeth Shippen Green joins Pyle's class and begins her friendship with Smith.

1896 Violet Oakley joins Pyle's class and befriends Smith and Green.

1897 *Evangeline,* with illustrations by Smith and Oakley, published.
Rents a studio and apartments at 1523 Chestnut Street, which she shares with Oakley and Jessie Dowd, another Pyle student.
Green joins the women in the new quarters after completing a tour of Europe.

1900 Spends summer with Oakley and Green at Bryn Mawr.

1901 Begins a one year lease on the Red Rose Inn, where she lives with Oakley, Green, and Henrietta Cozens.

1902–Wins Bronze Medal at the Charleston (South Carolina) Exposition.
Collaborates with Green on the Bryn Mawr College Calendar.

1903–Collaborates with Green on another calendar, *The Child,* which is later published as *The Book of the Child,* a work which brings both women national attention.
Wins the Mary Smith Prize for works exhibited at the Pennsylvania Academy of the Fine Arts.

1904–Wins Silver Medal for illustration at the St. Louis International Exposition.

1905 Red Rose Inn sold to H. S. Kerbaugh, who evicts the artist occupants. Mr. and Mrs. George Woodward, Chestnut Hill landowners refurbish Hill Farm for use of the artists as home and studios.

The new home is named Cogslea by the women.

1907 Exhibits her work with that of Oakley and Green at the Society of Illustrators exhibit at Waldorf Astoria.

1908 *Dream Blocks* is published, a popular collection of illustrations.

1911 Wins the Beck Prize at the Philadelphia Watercolor Club Exhibit held at the Academy.

Exhibits works at the Rome Exposition.

1911 Green marries Huger Elliott and leaves Cogslea. Smith purchases one acre of land from the Woodwards and begins to plan her home and studio, Cogshill.

1914 Cogshill completed. Moves to her new home with her brother, an aunt, and Henrietta Cozens.

1915 Exhibits at the Panama/Pacific Exposition in San Francisco and wins the watercolor medal.

1916 Dodd, Mead publishes *Water Babies*.

1917 December. Her first *Good Housekeeping* cover appears.

1918 Designs poster for the Red Cross and paints portraits for the U.S. Government's Division of Pictorial Publicity.

1923 Participates in a memorial exhibit of works by students of Howard Pyle.

1925 Increases her portrait painting activities, devoting less time to book and magazine illustration.

1927 Violet Oakley leaves for three years in Europe.

1933 Sails for Europe with a nurse and Isabel Crowder, a niece of Henrietta Cozens.

1935 May 3. Dies in Philadelphia, at her home, Cogshill.

1936 March 14 – April 12. Memorial Exhibit of her works held at the Pennsylvania Academy of the Fine Arts.

B · Illustrated Books

Nearly 40 books featuring illustrations by Jessie Willcox Smith were published during her lifetime. The following bibliography lists only the first edition of each work. Reprints of her more popular books were made frequently, many times in incomplete form, lacking some illustrations. In some cases, the works listed here contain only one or two illustrations or a cover illustration, and these are indicated.

Works are arranged chronologically and, when possible, special features of the edition are indicated.

Evangeline: A Tale of Acadie by Henry Wadsworth Longfellow, New York and Boston: Houghton Mifflin & Company, The Riverside Press, 1897. Five color chromolithograph illustrations by Smith, five by Oakley. Two-color headpieces by Smith.

The Head of a Hundred by Maud Wilder Goodwin, Boston: Little, Brown & Company, 1900. Five black and white plates.

Tales and Sketches by Nathaniel Hawthorne, Boston: Houghton Mifflin and Company, 1900 (Old Manse edition, The Complete Writings of Nathaniel Hawthorne, vol. 16). One black and white plate.

Mosses from an Old Manse by Nathaniel Hawthorne, Boston: Houghton Mifflin & Company, 1900 (Old Manse edition, The Complete Writings of Nathaniel Hawthorne, vol. 5). Frontispiece.

Brenda, Her School and Her Club by Helen Leah Reed, Boston: Houghton Mifflin & Company, 1900. Five black and white plates.

Brenda's Summer at Rockley by Helen Leah Reed, Boston: Little, Brown & Company, 1901. Five black and white plates.

An Old Fashioned Girl by Louisa May Alcott, Boston: Little, Brown & Company, 1902. Twelve black and white plates.

The Book of the Child by Mabel Humphrey, New York: Frederick A. Stokes Company, 1903. Illustrations originally published in 1902 for *The Child*, a calendar by Smith and Green. Three full color illustrations by Smith, three by Green. Cover by Smith, frontispiece by Green. Marginal red and black drawings by Smith.

Rhymes of Real Children by Elizabeth Sage Goodwin, New York: Fox, Duffield & Company, 1903. Seven full color plates, plus two color marginal drawings.

In the Closed Room by Frances Hodgson Burnett, New York: McClure, Phillips & Company, 1904. Eight full color illustrations, plus marginal decorations.

A Child's Garden of Verses by Robert Louis Stevenson, New York: Scribner's

(Scribner's Illustrated Classics), 1905. Ten full color plates, line drawings, decorated end papers, and color insert on front cover.

Billy Boy by John Luther Long, New York: Dodd, Mead and Company, 1906. Full color frontispiece, three black and white illustrations, and color insert on cover.

The Bed Time Book by Helen Hay Whitney, New York: Duffield & Company 1907.

Thirty Favourite Paintings, New York: P. F. Collier & Son, 1908. One color plate.

Dream Blocks by Aileen C. Higgins, New York: Duffield & Company, 1908. Twelve full color plates, line drawings, decorated end papers, color insert on cover.

The Seven Ages of Childhood, verses by Carolyn Wells, New York: Moffat, Yard & Company, 1909. Seven full color plates, decorated end papers, color insert on cover.

Sonny's Father by Ruth McEnery Stuart, New York: Century, 1910. Two black and white plates.

A Child's Book of Old Verses compiled by Jessie Willcox Smith, New York: Duffield & Company, 1910. Ten full color plates, marginal line drawings.

The Five Senses by Angela M. Keyes, New York: Moffat, Yard & Company, 1911. Five full color plates.

The Now-A-Days Fairy Book by Anna Alice Chapin, New York: Dodd & Company, 1911. Six full color plates.

A Child's Book of Stories compiled by Penrhyn Wingfield Coussens, New York: Duffield & Company, 1911.

Dickens' Children, Ten Children by Jessie Willcox Smith, New York: Charles Scribner's & Sons, 1912. Ten full color plates, color insert and gold stamping on cover.

'Twas the Night Before Christmas by Clement Clark Moore, Boston and New York: Houghton Mifflin & Company, 1912. Ten full color plates, one double page plate in color. Two color title page and decorated end papers.

American Art by American Artists, New York: Collier & Son, 1914. Two full color plates, three black and white plates.

Little Women by Louisa May Alcott, Boston: Little, Brown & Company, 1915. Eight full color plates.

A Child's Stamp Book of Old Verses pictured by Jessie Willcox Smith, New York: Duffield & Company, 1915. Twelve full color picture stamps. Two color cover with one picture stamp.

The Everyday Fairy Book by Anna Alice Chapin, New York: Dodd, Mead & Company, 1915.

When Christmas Comes Around by Priscilla Underwood, New York: Duffield & Company, 1915.

The Little Mother Goose by Jessie Willcox Smith, New York: Dodd, Mead & Company, 1915. Twelve full color plates, line drawings, color insert on cover.

The Water Babies by Charles Kingsley, New York: Dodd, Mead, & Company, 1916. Eight full color plates, two color marginal decorations, line drawings.

The Way to Wonderful by Mary Stewart Sheldon, New York: Dodd, Mead, & Company, 1917.

At the Back of the North Wind by George MacDonald, Philadelphia: David McKay Company, 1920, (McKay's Illustrated Classics). Eight full color plates, color title page.

The Princess and the Goblin by George MacDonald Philadelphia: David McKay Company, 1921 (McKay's Illustrated Classics). Eight full color plates, color title page.

A Child's Book of Modern Stories compiled by Ada M. Skinner and Eleanor Skinner, New York: Duffield & Company, 1920. Eight full color plates.

Heidi by Johanna Spyri, Philadelphia: David McKay Company, 1922 (McKay's Illustrated Classics). Eleven full color plates, full color title page, decorated end papers, marginal line drawings, color insert on cover.

A Little Child's Book of Stories compiled by Ada M. Skinner and Eleanor L. Skinner, New York: Duffield & Company, 1922. Ten full color plates.

A Very Little Child's Book of Stories compiled by Ada M. Skinner and Eleanor L. Skinner, New York: Duffield & Company, 1923. Eight full color plates, color insert on cover.

Boys and Girls of Bookland by Nora Archibald Smith, Philadelphia: David McKay Company, 1923. Eleven full color plates, color insert on cover.

The Children of Dickens compiled by Samuel McChord Crothers, New York: Scribner's, 1925 (Scribner's Illustrated Classics). Ten color plates, decorated end papers by Euphane Mallison, color insert on cover.

A Child's Prayer by Cora Cassard Toogood, Philadelphia: David McKay Company, 1925. Six color line drawings, full color insert on cover.

A Child's Book of Country Stories by Ada Marie Skinner and Eleanor Skinner, New York: Duffield & Company, 1925. Five full color illustrations.

Kitchen Fun – A Cookbook for Children by Louise Price Bell, Cleveland: Harter Publishing Company, 1932. Full color insert on cover.

C · Magazine Covers and Illustrations

Jessie Willcox Smith was best known to her admirers for her ever-present magazine covers which appeared in clockwork fashion throughout her long career. In some instances, her covers were reprints of illustrations she had originally drawn for children's books, but in most cases the following illustrations were designed exclusively for magazine cover use.

The list of publications is arranged alphabetically with covers listed chronologically under the magazine title. Most covers are untitled, but titles have been included when they are available.

Collier's Weekly
October 18, 1899, "Indian Summer"
January 3, 1903
April 2, 1904, "Easter"
April 30, 1904, "The May Pole"
June 25, 1904
July 30, 1904
August 27, 1904
September 24, 1904, "Autumn Days"
October 26, 1904.
December 3, 1904, "The First Day at School"
February 25, 1905
March 25, 1905
April 29, 1905, "The Secret"
May 27, 1905
June 24, 1905
July 29, 1905
August 26, 1905
September 16, 1905, "The Hayloft"
September 30, 1905
November 25, 1905, "The Northwest Passage"
December 23, 1905
December 30, 1905, "Billy Boy"
January 27, 1906
February 24, 1906, "Tragedies of Childhood – The Popular Cut"

March 31, 1906
April 7, 1906, "His Easter Lily"
April 28, 1906, "Tragedies of Childhood – The Hurt Finger"
May 26, 1906, "A Tempered Wind"
May 31, 1906, "Tragedies of Childhood – A Broken Head and Heart"
June 30, 1906
July 28, 1906, "The Land of Counterpane"
September 29, 1906, "The Comedies of Childhood – Peep-Bo!"
November 24, 1906, "The Comedies of Childhood – Jack in the Box"
December 15, 1906, "Christmas"
January 26, 1907, "Tragedies of Childhood – Lost"
March 16, 1907, "The March Wind"
June 29, 1907, "She Lufs Me – She Lufs Me Not"
September 18, 1907, "Little Heroines of Fairy Tales – Goldilocks"
October 5, 1907, "The Helper"
December 21, 1907, "Twas the Night Before Christmas"
December 28, 1907, "The Sewing Lesson"
January 25, 1908, "Give Me Leave"
April 11, 1914
December 9, 1916

The Delineator
June, 1915, "Little Women"

Good Housekeeping
December, 1917 through March, 1933

Harper's Young People
April 12, 1892, "His First Easter"

House and Garden
June, 1931

The Independent
December 6, 1915, "Little Women"

The Ladies' Home Journal
May, 1904
October, 1904
December, 1904, "The First Lesson"
January, 1905, "The First Punishment"
March, 1905, "The First Love"
April, 1905, "The First Sermon"
July, 1905, "The First Dissipation"
November, 1912, "A Child's Grace"
December, 1914, "Tiny Tim"
August, 1915

McClure's Magazine
January, 1904
August, 1904
December, 1909

Red Cross Magazine
December, 1918

Scribner's Magazine
August, 1900

Woman's Home Companion
August, 1898
December, 1907
December, 1910
September, 1911
July, 1912
November, 1912
December, 1913
December, 1915
September, 1920
October, 1920

Illustrations

The following listing gathers together Smith's illustrations appearing in numerous publications, either singly or as part of an illustrated article or story. Titles refer to the illustration or its series or the title of the accompanying text. The list of publications is arranged alphabetically with illustrations chronologically ordered under each title.

Appleton's Magazine
May, 1908, "Must Your Child Lie?" by G. Stanley Hall

Century Magazine
December, 1902, "While the Mother Works: A Look At the Day Nurseries of New York"
May, 1904, "Spring" from Goethe's Prose by Alice Williams Brotherton

Collier's Weekly
November 26, 1904, frontispiece
December 3, 1904, frontispiece, "Christmas Eve"
December 31, 1904, frontispiece, "Kept In"
April 15, 1905, "Foreign Children"
May 13, 1905, frontispiece, "The Recitation"
December 16, 1905, poem, "Chums" by J. W. Foley
December 16, 1905, "Rasselas in the Vegetable Kingdom" by Georgia Wood Pangborn
December 23, 1905, "The Signs of the States"
December 30, 1905, "Billy Boy," by John Luther Long
April 7, 1906, "A Pillar of Society" by Josephine Bacon

April 7, 1906, frontispiece, "His Easter Lily"
April 26, 1906, "A Tempered Wind" by G. W. Pangborn
July 28, 1906, frontispiece, "The Land of Counterpane"
October 6, "Out of the House of Bondage," by Grace MacGowan Cooke
December 15, 1906, "Ladybird," by Edith Barnard
December 22, 1906, "Bed in Summer," by Robert L. Stevenson
September 28, 1907, "Goldilocks and the Three Bears"
December 14, 1907, "The Process of the Blest" by J. W. Foley
December 21, 1907, " 'Twas the Night Before Christmas"
May 30, 1908, "Beauty and the Beast"
December 12, 1908, "A Modern Cinderella"
November 20, 1909, "Little Red Riding Hood"
December 11, 1909, frontispiece, "Caught in the Act"
June 11, 1910, "Sleeping Beauty"
December 23, 1915, "The Signs of the Stars" by Owen Oliver
December 23, 1915, reprint of "The Procession of the Blest"

Frank Leslie's Popular Monthly [*American Magazine*)
February, 1903, "The Pettison Firsts" by Marion Hill
March, 1903, "A Princess Listens" by Roy Rolfe Gilson
August, 1903, "Within the Ring of Singing: A Story of the Pettison Twins."
   by Marion Hill

Good Housekeeping
December, 1912, "Pease Porridge Hot, Pease Porridge Cold"
January, 1913, "Little Miss Muffet"
February, 1913, "See, Saw, Marjery Daw"
March, 1913, "The Way to London Town"
April, 1913, "Rain, Rain, Go Away"
May, 1913, "The Old Woman Who Lived in a Shoe"
June, 1913, "Mary, Mary, Quite Contrary"
July, 1913
August, 1913, "Jack and Jill"
September, 1913, "Rock-a-bye Baby, on the Tree Top"
October, 1913, "A Dillar, A Dollar, A Ton O'Clock Scholar"
November, 1913, "Peter, Peter, Pumpkin Eater"
December, 1913, "Little Jack Horner"
January, 1914, "Curly Locks, Curly Locks"
February, 1914, "Polly Put the Kettle On"
March, 1914, "Round the Ring of Roses"
April, 1914, "Hot Cross Buns"
March, 1916, "Mothers and Children" by Louise Hogan
September, 1916, "What Really Happened" by Dorothy Canfield
February, 1917, "Betty Manifests the Spirit" by Claudia Cranston

Harper's Bazaar
November, 1902, "The Twilight of Life"
March, 1903, "Two Careers"
May, 1903, "The Story Hour"
December, 1912, "The Embarrassment of Riches"

Harper's Monthly Magazine
May, 1903, "An Idealist" by Netta Syrett
June, 1903, "As You Sailed," by Roy Rolfe Gilson

Harper's Round Table
April 14, 1891, "Nursery Weather Signals"

Harper's Weekly
December 6, 1902, "Little Paul's Christ Child" by Kathryn Jarboes
October 3, 1903, "Diversions of the Higher Journalist, A new Evil"

The Ladies' Home Journal
November, 1905, "A Child's Good-Night Bed Quilt.
April, 1907, "The Little White Bear" by Emerson Taylor
November, 1908, "The Seven Ages of Childhood – First the Infant in his
    Mother's Arms." by Carolyn Wells
December, 1908, "The Seven Ages of Childhood – Then the Toddling Baby
    Boy, with Shining Morning Face, Creeping Like a Snail" by Carolyn Wells
January, 1909, "The Seven Ages of Childhood – Then the Epicure, with Fine
    and Greedy Taste for Porridge" by Carolyn Wells
March, 1909, "The Seven Ages of Childhood – Then the Lover, Sighing Like
    a Furnace" by Carolyn Wells
April, 1909, "The Seven Ages of Childhood – Then the Scholar, with Eyes
    Severe and Hair of Formal Cut" by Carolyn Wells
August, 1909, "The Seven Ages of Childhood – Then the Lean and Thoughtful
    Maiden, with Dreaming Eyes and Quiet Mien" by Carolyn Wells
September, 1909, "The Seven Ages of Childhood – Last Scene of All That ends
    This eventful History is First Love and Mere Enchantment, Sans Mother,
    Sans Father, Sans Brother, Sans Everything" by Carolyn Wells
October, 1926, "You Must Eat Certain Food Because They are Good for You
    Whether You Like Them or Not"

The Literary Digest International Book Review
November, 1932, "More Books in the Home"

McClure's Magazine
August, 1903, "The Method of Charles Stuart York" by May Kelsey Champion
August, 1904, "In the Closed Room, Part 1" by Frances Hodgson Burnett
September, 1904, "In the Closed Room, Part 2" by Frances Hodgson Burnett
February, 1905, Frontispiece

April, 1905, "A Social Event," by Florence Tinsley Cox
November, 1905, "Night, and the Curtains Drawn," by Justus Miles Forman
October, 1907, "The Five Senses"
December, 1909, "A Child's World"

Publisher's Weekly
August 4, 1923, "More Books in the Home!"

Saint Nicholas Magazine
May, 1888, "Five Little Maidens All in a Row" by Jessie Willcox Smith
May, 1891, "Dorothy, Dorcas, and Dill" by Jessie Willcox Smith
December, 1901, "Little Puritans" by Ethel Parton

Scribner's Magazine
December, 1900, "The Emigrant East" by Arthur Colton
December, 1900, "The Child" by Bertha Gerneaux Woods
December, 1901, "The Last of the Fairy Wands" by William Henry Bishop
December, 1902, "A Mother's Days"
April, 1903, "The Blue Dress" by Josephine Daskom
May, 1903, "Kitchen Sketches" by Elizabeth Hale Gilman
December, 1903, "The Child in a Garden"
March, 1904, "Home Sketches" by Elizabeth Hale Gilman
December, 1911, "Dickens' Children"
August, 1912, "Dickens' Children"
January, 1915, "Kipling's Children"

Woman's Home Companion
November, 1908, "The Better Treasure" by Mary Raymond Shipman Andrews
December, 1909, "Families Verses of Childhood – Twinkle, Twinkle Little Star"
March, 1910, "Familiar Verses of Childhood – How Doth the Little Busy Bee"
May, 1910, "Familiar Verses of Childhood – Let Dogs Delight to Bark and Bite"
September, 1910, "Familiar Verses of Childhood – The Goose Girl"
November, 1910, "Diamond sat down again, took the baby on his lap"
April, 1913, "Hansel and Gretel"
September, 1913, "Cinderella"
October, 1913, "Goldilocks"
April, 1914, "Jack and the Beanstalk"
November, 1915, "Snow White"
January, 1917, "When Music, Heavenly Maid, Was Young" by Arthur Guiterman
December, 1919, "My Ball of Twine" by Josephine Fishburn

D·Posters, Calendars, Miscellaneous Works

Posters and calendars were rare products of Smith's imagination. In some cases, creative publishers took illustrations from her illustrated books and other sources and adapted them to calendar or poster use. The following listing is designed to aid collectors in searching for and identifying these unusual items.

1902 *Bryn Mawr College Calendar for* 1902, $6\frac{1}{4}'' \times 13\frac{3}{4}''$. Illustrations by Smith and Green. Bryn Mawr, Pennsylvania: Bryn Mawr College. Two color lithography.

1902 *The Child, A Calendar for* 1902, Philadelphia: C. W. Beck and Company. Full color illustrations by Smith and Elizabeth Shippen Green. $13\frac{3}{4}'' \times 15''$.

1912 *Children of Dickens, A Calendar for* 1912, New York: Charles Scribners & Sons. Four full color illustrations.

1918 poster, *Have You a Red Cross Service Flag?* Washington, D.C.: National Red Cross. Full Color, $20'' \times 30''$.

1919 poster, *This Simple Faith has Made America Great,* Washington, D.C.: Interchurch World Movement, Full color, $21'' \times 28''$.

1919 poster, *Children's Book Week, November 10th to 15th,* 1919. New York: American Association of Book Publishers. Full color, $14\frac{1}{2}'' \times 23''$.

1922 poster, *Children's Book Week,* New York: American Association of Book Publishers. Full color, $14\frac{1}{2}'' \times 23''$.

1923 poster, *More Books in the Home,* New York: American Association of Book Publishers. Full color, $14\frac{1}{2}'' \times 23''$.

1924 *Suppose Nobody Cared?* York: Philadelphia Welfare Federation. Full Color, $25'' \times 39''$.

1925 *Give,* Philadelphia Welfare Federation. Full color, $25'' \times 39''$.

1926 poster, *Somebody Cares. Do You?* Philadelphia Welfare Federation. Full color, $25'' \times 39''$.

1927 poster, *Give,* Philadelphia Welfare Federation. Full color, $25'' \times 39''$

Notes

1. Christine Jones Huber, *The Pennsylvania Academy and Its Women* (Philadelphia: Pennsylvania Academy of the Fine Arts, 1973). pp. 19-20.
2. "Miss Beaux in her Studio," unsigned, Violet Oakley's Scrapbook (New York: Archives of American Art, October, 1898).
3. Ibid.
4. Regina Armstrong, "Representative Women Illustrators: The Child Interpreters," *The Critic* (May, 1900) p. 417.
5. *Report of the Private View of the Exhibition of Works by Howard Pyle at the Art Alliance:* Philadelphia, January 22, 1923 (Philadelphia: Ad Service Printing Company, 1923) p. 19.
6. Howard Pyle, Introduction to *Evangeline: A Tale of Acadie* by Henry Wadsworth Longfellow (Boston and New York: Houghton Mifflin & Company, 1897) p. xix.
7. *Report of the Private View of the Exhibition,* p. 19.
8. Smith to Sartain, 17 May 1900, Pennsylvania Academy of the Fine Arts.
9. Interview with Edith Emerson, September 7, 1976.
10. "Jessie Willcox Smith," *The New York Times* (May 4, 1935).
11. Mary Haeseler Dougherty, "Peter Pan's Portrait Painter," *The Philadelphia Public Ledger* (July 16, 1922).
12. Jessie Willcox Smith, "Jessie Willcox Smith," *Good Housekeeping* (October, 1917) p. 25.
13. Interview with Mrs. William S. Crowder (former Isabel Lewis), November 30, 1976.
14. Jessie Willcox Smith, *Good Housekeeping,* p. 24.
15. Ibid. p. 24.
16. Interview, Edith Emerson.
17. Huber, *The Pennsylvania Academy and Its Women,* p. 21.
18. Interview, Edith Emerson.
19. Dougherty, "Peter Pan's Portrait Painter."
20. Smith, *Good Housekeeping,* 24.
21. Anonymous, untitled clipping, Violet Oakley's scrapbook, New York: Archives of American Art, undated.
22. Friendship Calendar, 1900, given to Jessie H. Dowd. Collection of Mrs. William S. Crowder.
23. "Anthony Drexel Buys Red Rose Inn," *The Philadelphia Press* (October 24, 1901).
24. Ibid.
25. Inscription in *The Lure of the Garden,* collection of Mrs. William S. Crowder.
26. Catalog, 64th Annual Exhibit, Pennsylvania Academy of the Fine Arts (December 17, 1894 – February 23, 1895).
27. Interview, Edith Emerson.
28. Ibid.
29. Ibid.
30. Merrick to Schnessel, 13 October 1976.
31. Ibid.
32. Edith Emerson, "Jessie Willcox Smith, An Appreciation," *Catalog of the Memorial Exhibition of the Work of Jessie Willcox Smith* (Philadelphia: Pennsylvania Academy of the Fine Arts, March 14 – April 12, 1936).
33. Smith, *Good Housekeeping,* p. 190.
34. Henry C. Pitz, *Howard Pyle, Writer, Illustrator, Founder of the Brandywine School* (New York: Clarkson N. Potter, 1975) p. 38.

35. Ibid. p. 135.

36. Charles DeFeo in *Howard Pyle, Diversity in Depth,* (Wilmington: The Delaware Art Museum, March 5 – April 15, 1973).

37. Charles D. Abbott, *Howard Pyle – A Chronicle* (New York and London: Harper and Brothers, 1925), p. vi.

38. Mary Tracy Earle, "The Red Rose," *The Lamp,* (May, 1903), p. 278.

39. Pitz, Howard Pyle, p. 138.

40. Brown to Thornton Oakley, 15 July 1947, Free Library of Philadelphia.

41. Friendship Calendar given to Dowd.

42. Interview, Mrs. William S. Crowder.

43. Interview, Edith Emerson.

44. "New Capitol Plans in Full Detail Announced," *The Philadelphia Free Press,* Violet Oakley's scrapbook, New York: Archives of American Art, undated article.

45. Ibid.

46. Interview, Edith Emerson.

47. Inscription in a book given to Pierre M. Purves, Christmas, 1914. Collection, Pierre M. Purves.

48. George Alfred Williams, "American Painters of Children," *Woman's Home Companion* (September, 1911) p. 14.

49. Elizabeth Lore North, "Women Illustrators of Child Life," *Outlook* (October 1, 1904) p. 271.

50. Edith Emerson, "The Age of Innocence," *The American Magazine of Art* (July, 1925) p. 345.

51. Smith, *Good Housekeeping,* p. 190.

52. Ibid. p. 190.

53. Edward T. James, ed. *Notable American Women, 1607-1950* (Cambridge: Harvard University, The Belknap Press) 1971.

54. *Collier's* (October 14, 1905) p. 21.

55. Oakley to Robert Underwood Johnson, *Century* Publications (8 January 1904), New York: Archives of American Art.

56. Smith to Robert Underwood Johnson, *Century* Publications (25 March 1910 to 6 October 1912), New York: Archives of American Art.

57. Ibid. (25 March 1910).

58. Ibid. (28 July 1912).

59. Ibid. (22 September 1912).

60. Ibid. (22 September 1912).

61. Rilla Evelyn Jackman, *American Arts* (Chicago: Rand McNally & Co.) p. 254.

62. Jessie Trimble, "Studying and Succeeding in Art," *New Idea Woman's Magazine* 14 (1906), p. 14.

63. Regina Armstrong, "Representative American Women Illustrators – The Decorative Workers," *The Critic* (June, 1900) p. 523.

64. Interview, Edith Emerson.

65. Percy V. Bradshaw, *Art in Advertising* (London: The Press Art School, 1925) p. 486.

66. Edith Emerson, Introduction to *Portraits, Drawings, and Illustrations by Jessie Willcox Smith,* Philadelphia: The Art Alliance, 1924.

67. Smith, *Good Housekeeping,* p. 24.

68. Ibid, p. 193.

69. Ibid, p. 190.

70. Interview with Mrs. Herbert J. Goldbloom, November 10, 1976.

71. Emerson, "The Age of Innocence," p. 355.

72. Dougherty, "Peter Pan's Portrait Painter."

73. Emerson, "The Age of Innocence," p. 345.

74. Ibid. p. 345.

75. Smith, *Good Housekeeping,* p. 193.

Index

Produced by James J. Kery
Designer: Ian Craig
Consulting editors: Pat Kery, Richard Page, Peter Ward

Set in 12 pt. Garamond 156, 2pts. leaded
Paper: 115 gsm Bucaneer Matt Coated Cartridge, 115 gsm Oberon Art.
Printed and bound in Great Britain by
Morrison and Gibb Ltd., London and Edinburgh